SPORT IS
THE ANSWER

by Chris Coley and Paul Clixby

All profits from the sale of this book will be shared by
The Injured Jockeys Fund and Acorns Children's Hospice

Copyright © Chris Coley and Paul Clixby 2020
ISBN 978-1-5272-6180-8
A catalogue record for this book is available from the British Library
All rights reserved. No part of this publication may be copied, reproduced or transmitted in any form
or by any means without the prior written permission of the publishers

Foreword by Harry Redknapp

Chris Coley and I share the same two sporting passions, football and horse racing. I first came across Chris some three years ago when he made me an offer I simply could not afford to refuse and that was to be the Manager of the Jockeys XI in the inaugural Injured Jockeys Fund match against a Cheltenham Town Legends XI. Finalising the offer took much negotiation but, with the contract having been passed backwards and forwards between various high-powered lawyers, I did duly accept and the deal was signed!

HOWEVER, on the day of the game, and with racing at Cheltenham scheduled for that very same afternoon, out of the blue Birmingham City ("The Blues" – ironically Chris' team!) came along with a somewhat better offer begging me to motivate the team to somehow win two of their final three Championship games to save them from relegation! They then called a press conference for that same evening and instead of being at Whaddon Rd I was in front of the cameras in Birmingham.... Charlie George kindly stepped in for Chris at short notice and along with Rod Thomas they did an excellent job I'm told, both in the dugout and an even better job in the bar afterwards, and even later into the night at the Hotel du Vin.

However last year there were no last minute hitches and I duly had a great afternoon's racing at Prestbury Park and then headed down the road to the Cheltenham ground to meet up with the legendary AP and his fellow jockeys, most of whom had been riding in the afternoon!

The team surprised me with their skills: David Bass showing great pace, Jamie Bargary with the touch of a real pro, Wayne Hutchinson a true class act with time galore on the ball, trainer Ben Pauling a rock in defence and AP controlling the game from midfield, reminding me of Liam Brady. Sam Twiston-Davies, certainly blessed with two, let alone one, left feet had no idea of any positional sense whatsoever and roamed aimlessly, and at last, wonder of wonders, Robbie Dunne did finally consent to pass the ball... but the match was duly won and there was fun and merriment in the bar afterwards, particularly with the opposing manager, Nicky Henderson, wearing his Unibet hat.

And since the game I now find myself in partnership with Chris in two horses at Fergal O'Brien's (please don't anyone tell Sandra!) and our dreams are very much alive, with a runner at the recent Festival, and plenty more to come, I hope!

I trust you enjoy the book and find it not just full of boring old facts, but fun and entertaining too. Please read on and keep, keep, keep dreaming in these troubled times of either that magic winning goal at Wembley or, even better now perhaps, of one of our horses winning the Gold Cup at Cheltenham!

CONTENTS

Each round has a theme, which should give you a clue to some answers. A few rounds have extra instructions at the beginning.
All answers have been researched as correct as at 1 May 2020.

ROUND		PAGE
1	UNDER STARTER'S ORDERS - A MIXED BAG	1
2	LIFE ON THE OCEAN WAVES	2
3	THE LUCK OF THE IRISH	3
4	WHEN THE SAINTS GO MARCHING IN	4
5	VIEW FROM THE STANDS	5
6	UP THE GARDEN PATH	6
7	KEEPING UP WITH THE JONESES	7
8	FOOD GLORIOUS FOOD	8
9	THE FRENCH CONNECTION	9
10	I WAS THERE (PAUL'S OWN REMINISCENCES)	10
11	LIKE FATHER LIKE SON	11
12	WEIGHTS AND MEASURES	12
13	FIRST IMPRESSIONS	13
14	GENUINE ALL-ROUNDERS	14
15	FOR THOSE WATCHING IN BLACK AND WHITE	15
16	GIANT KILLERS AND UNDERDOGS	16
17	AUSSIE RULES	17
18	PASSPORT CONTROL	18
19	TAKE YOUR PARTNERS	19
20	HOLY ORDERS	20
21	FACE THE MUSIC	21
22	CHRISTIAN NAMES/SURNAMES	22
23	SURNAMES/CHRISTIAN NAMES	23
24	MAMMA MIA	24
25	ANOTHER DOOR OPENS	25
26	ROGUES AND VILLAINS	26
27	JOB DESCRIPTIONS	27
28	TEN TO ONE	28
29	CASH IS KING	29
30	WHERE IN THE COUNTRY	30
31	A GOOD READ	31
32	THE AMERICAN DREAM	32
33	TOWNS AND CITIES IN THE UK	33
34	OVER THE HILLS AND FAR AWAY	34
35	BROTHERLY LOVE	35
36	THE NUMBERS BOARD	36
37	IT'S A DOG'S LIFE	37
38	THE SMITHS	38
39	CAPTAIN MARVELS	39
40	COMPASS POINTS	40
41	THE SILVER SCREEN	41
42	HOT STREAKS	42
43	I CAN NEVER DO CRYPTIC CROSSWORDS	43

44	CACKHANDERS	44
45	KEEP YOUR HEAD ABOVE WATER	45
46 - 55	**HALF-TIME ENTERTAINMENT**	46
56	NO MAN IS AN ISLAND	47
57	LAND OF MY FATHERS	48
58	WHERE WOULD YOU BE?	49
59	MORE GENUINE ALL-ROUNDERS	50
60	TURN OF THE CENTURY	51
61	INITIALS FOR SPORTING PHRASES	52
62	THE SILVER SCREEN – THE SEQUEL	53
63	INJURY TIME	54
64	AUF WIEDERSEHEN PET	55
65	AROUND THE HOUSE	56
66	THE COMMENTATOR'S CURSE	57
67	THE SPORTING DICTIONARY	58
68	AND IN THE BEGINNING	59
69	ANCIENT AND MODERN	60
70	SCOTLAND THE BRAVE	61
71	SPORTING DISASTERS	62
72	KEEP IT IN THE FAMILY	63
73	DID IT REALLY HAPPEN?	64
74	DOWN ON THE FARM	65
75	CENTRAL EUROPE	66
76	CAN'T SEE THE WOOD FOR THE TREES	67
77	PIPPED AT THE POST	68
78	THE WHEEL OF FORTUNE	69
79	TOP OF THE CLASS	70
80	THE SPANISH INQUISITION	71
81	WAY BACK IN TIME	72
82	GONE FISHIN'	73
83	FILM/TV – THE NAME'S THE SAME	74
84	MARITAL BLISS	75
85	"AND I QUOTE"	76
86	THE DRINKS CABINET	77
87	STRANGE BUT TRUE	78
88	YOUR SATNAV MIGHT HELP	79
89	THE NOBILITY	80
90	I WAS THERE (CHRIS'S OWN REMINISCENCES)	81
91	THE MET OFFICE	82
92	MRS BROWN'S BOYS	83
93	LONDON CALLING	84
94	OUT OF AFRICA	85
95	I CAN SEE CLEARLY NOW	86
96	THE QUEEN'S CORONATION YEAR	87
97	WHEN THERE WAS STILL SPORT IN 2020	88
98	THE NHS	89
99	THE LAST GOODBYES	90
100	THE FINISHING POST - A MIXED BAG	91

ANSWERS 93-99

1. UNDER STARTER'S ORDERS - A MIXED BAG

1. Which cricketer with over 700 Test wickets had after his first two Tests remarkably taken just 1-335?

2. The Isle of Man TT races are an annual motorcycling event. What does TT stand for?

3. What is the only country other than Greece to have competed at every "modern" Olympic games?

4. Sunderland did it in 1979, Villa did it in 1981, but who did it in 1980?

5. Joe Marler faced disciplinary action after the 2020 Six Nations for allegedly grabbing which player's genitals?

6. Which former champion flat jockey rode the winner of the 1982 Cheshire Oaks at Chester in between his wedding and the wedding reception?

7. Which Formula One racing driver, still competing in 2019, holds the record of 177 races without ever finishing in a podium position?

8. According to Greek mythology the god Apollo killed his lover Hyacinthus while practising what?

9. Who beat Ivan Lendl in the 1989 French Open tennis championship using unorthodox tactics including an under-arm serve?

10. In the 1994-95 season at which Premier League club was Brian Little managing Bryan Small?

2. LIFE ON THE OCEAN WAVES

1. Which winger was a member of the Australian side who won the rugby league World Cup in 2000, and then turned to rugby union, winning a further 37 International caps?

2. If the "Seagulls" were playing football against the "Shrimpers", which two teams would be competing?

3. Dame De Compagnie, owned by JP McManus, won which race at the 2020 Cheltenham Festival?

4. Horse Guards Parade was the somewhat unlikely venue for which sport at the 2012 London Olympics?

5. Who was the Australian boxer, called by the Americans "the boxer with the educated left hand", who was negotiating to fight Sugar Ray Robinson for the world middleweight title, when suddenly Randolph Turpin took the fight and beat Sugar Ray?

6. Near what bridge do the runners in the Grand National cross the Melling Road when they are said to be "re-entering the racecourse proper"?

7. Which Premiership rugby union side play at the AJ Bell Stadium?

8. Who was the joint master of the South Shropshire Hunt, and the son of a Roxy Music star, who in 2004 illegally entered Parliament from behind the Speaker's Chair to disrupt a debate on fox hunting?

9. Which golfer, whose brother Gary is a high-profile pianist, composer and songwriter, won the 1982 Masters and produced a book entitled "I Am the Walrus: Confessions and Tips from a Blue Collar Golfer"?

10. Which NFL team play their home games at Hard Rock Stadium?

3. THE LUCK OF THE IRISH

1. Who originally came to England to be a jockey, but with weight problems decided to switch to snooker, where he twice won the world championships in 1972 and 1982, and was known as the "People's Champion"?

2. Who, with her victory over Delfine Persoon in 2019, became one of only seven boxers in history (male and female), to hold all four major world titles at the same weight simultaneously?

3. Which Irishman holds the Six Nations record for most tries scored with 26, and is the highest scoring centre of all time?

4. Which Irish racehorse trainer has trained three Grand National winners (in successive years, with different horses), four Cheltenham Gold Cup winners and six Epsom Derby winners?

5. Which cyclist in 1987 achieved a treble of victories in the Tour de France, the Giro d'Italia and the World Road Race championship?

6. Which Kilkenny player appeared in a record thirteen All Ireland Hurling Championship finals, winning ten of them between 2000 and 2014?

7. Where did Shane Lowry win the 2019 Open Golf championship, setting a new course record in the process?

8. Who was the last Irishman to win the BBC Sports Personality of the Year award?

9. Which Irishman at UFC 194 defeated Jose Aldo for the UFC Featherweight, doing so by knockout just 13 seconds into the first round – the fastest victory in a UFC championship fight?

10. Whose funeral in December 2005 attracted an estimated 100,000 mourners along the route, as his cortege moved the short distance from his family home to Stormont?

4. WHEN THE SAINTS GO MARCHING IN

1. Who scored the winning goal for Liverpool in the 1965 FA Cup final?

2. Who won the Open Golf championship the last time it was played at St Andrews in 2015?

3. Who is Northampton Saints' all-time record points scorer, who made his debut for the club in 1993? His son now plays for the Saints.

4. Where were the 1904 Summer Olympics held?

5. Who plays home games at the Totally Wicked Stadium?

6. Which US city has an ice hockey team called the Sharks, and a Major League soccer team called the Earthquakes?

7. What is Usain Bolt's middle name?

8. Which horse did Lester Piggott ride to victory in the 1960 Epsom Derby?

9. At which cricket ground did Brian Lara twice set the record for the highest individual Test innings?

10. In which Scottish city do St Johnstone football club play?

5. VIEW FROM THE STANDS

What sport would you be watching at:

1. Cowdray Park?
2. The Tony Macaroni Arena?
3. York Hall, Bethnal Green?
4. The Dringhouses Club, between the stables at York racecourse?
5. The Roodee?
6. Calshot?
7. The Dripping Pan?
8. Seaton Carew?
9. The Rose Bowl?
10. The Mend-a-Hose Jungle?

6. UP THE GARDEN PATH

1. Mike Atherton was given out LBW in the first over of which umpire's 66th and final Test match, a decision all the more surprising as he was not renowned for giving too many LBWs?

2. What major sporting stadium was once referred to as "Billy Williams' Cabbage Patch"?

3. What game uses two sets of seven coloured and numbered balls, with one black ball, and a white cue ball?

4. Who was the leading lady darts player in the 1980's, before becoming Phil Taylor's first manager?

5. Who was the defender who scored two goals for England against Panama at the 2018 FIFA World Cup?

6. Which horse ridden by Neville Sellwood won the Epsom Derby in 1962 – the race being marred when seven horses either fell or were brought down?

7. What is the affectionate local name for the terrace at the Kingsholm rugby union stadium, which stretches across the north side of the ground?

8. What is the nickname of the Swindon speedway team?

9. Which former England cricket coach holds the record for the highest ever Test score posted by a wicketkeeper batsman?

10. Which broadcaster presented various sports programmes on TV including Ski Sunday, A Question of Sport, The World Snooker Championships, as well as the Eurovision Song Contest and Miss World?

7. KEEPING UP WITH THE JONESES

1. Which golfer was the co-founder of the Masters, and is the only player in golf history to win all four Majors in the same calendar year?

2. Who is the world's most capped lock forward and Wales' most capped international player?

3. Which Australian Test cricketer retired with a first-class average of 51.85, and played in England for Durham and Derbyshire?

4. Which footballer, sent off 12 times in his career, holds the record for the quickest ever booking in a football match, being booked after just three seconds in an FA Cup tie between Chelsea and Sheffield United in 1992?

5. Who played club rugby for Neath and Llanelli in the early 1950's, representing both Wales and the British Lions; before switching codes to join Leeds, and also playing for Great Britain?

6. Which Welsh winger won 59 international caps, and was a member of Tottenham Hotspur's 1960-1961 double winning side?

7. Which Welsh taekwondo athlete won Olympic gold medals in both 2012 and 2016 in the women's 57kg category?

8. Which driver, whose father Stan had also won an Australian Grand Prix, was the 1980 Formula One champion?

9. Which wicketkeeper retired from first-class cricket in 2015, having played international cricket for both England and Papua New Guinea, and after playing many seasons for Kent, but later captaining Gloucestershire?

10. Who was the losing finalist in singles, doubles and mixed doubles at the world table tennis championships in 1957 but later, in 1969, won the Wimbledon Ladies Singles title?

8. FOOD GLORIOUS FOOD

1. England needed 17 off the final over bowled by Bruce Reid in a 1987 Benson and Hedges world series match but who was the England batsman who won the match with a ball to spare?

2. Who won the European, world and Olympic figure skating gold medals in 1976 who died at the age of 44 in the arms of actor Alan Bates having had an AIDS-related heart attack?

3. Which racehorse, foaled in Australia and ridden by Richard Pitman, carried top weight in the 1973 Grand National and was caught in the final strides by Red Rum, carrying 23lbs less weight?

4. Which basketball player, later to be an ordained minister, was for 22 years known as the 'Clown Prince' of the Harlem Globetrotters?

5. Cwm Rhondda is known as the 'Welsh rugby hymn' but by what name is it known in English?

6. Who in May 2012 stepped down from a professional relationship with Arsenal after a cumulative 44 years with the club as player, caretaker manager and assistant manager?

7. Which New Zealand born rugby player, who has played Super Rugby for the Crusaders, made his England international debut in August 2019 and one day later was named in the 31-man squad for the World Cup in Japan?

8. Wayne Shaw, a goalkeeper with Sutton United, was fined £375 and banned for two months by the FA in September 2017 for breaching their betting rules, involving an FA Cup match which Sutton lost 2-0 to Arsenal. But what particular food was involved in this incident?

9. Which England seam bowler took two Australian wickets with the very first two balls of the morning on the second day of the 2009 Edgbaston Test?

10. Which champion Australian racehorse, a filly, retired undefeated after 25 races in April 2013 having won 15 group one victories?

9. THE FRENCH CONNECTION

1. Who was known as "The Orchid Man"? He was an aviator during the First World War, who won the Croix de Guerre and the Medaille Militaire. After the war he lost a world heavyweight title fight to Jack Dempsey (they remained lifelong friends), became an actor and made three films in Hollywood.

2. Francis Karine Ruby was the first woman in 1998 to win a gold medal in which new Winter Olympic sport?

3. Which jockey rode 3,314 winners in his career, including four Prix de L'Arc de Triomphes, and is now an avid collector of vintage cars?

4. Which "kung fu" kicking footballer baffled a press conference with the words "When the seagulls follow the trawler, it's because they think sardines will be thrown into the sea. Thank you very much"?

5. Which cyclist was the first man to win the Tour de France five times?

6. Who, at Grenoble Winter Olympics in 1968, completed a remarkable treble when winning gold medals in the downhill, giant slalom and slalom races?

7. Which tennis player won five French Open ladies doubles titles, yet lost in six Wimbledon ladies doubles finals?

8. Who at the 2018 FIFA World Cup became the third man, after Mario Zagallo and Franz Beckenbauer, to win the FIFA World Cup as both player and manager?

9. At what sport, played over two days at the 1900 Paris Olympics, did England beat France?

10. Which flanker played rugby 59 times for France, captain on 34 occasions, and is now a renowned painter and sculptor, exhibiting all around the world?

10. I WAS THERE (PAUL'S OWN REMINISCENCES)

1. At Lord's in 2010 when Mohammad Amir bowled a no ball which would have massive repercussions for him and cricket in general. But which England player made his highest test score of 169 in that innings?

2. At Field Mill on 26 February 1969 when we stuffed* West Ham 3-0 (and they had all their three World Cup winners and other stars playing) to reach the FA Cup quarter finals for the only time in the club's history. Who was I supporting?

3. At Sixways for the last game of the 2004-05 Premiership when Worcester Warriors secured safety in their first season in the top flight with a win over Northampton. Which former Gloucester forward was Worcester's director of rugby at the time?

4. At the 2012 London Olympic triathlon. Where in the capital was it held?

5. At Trent Bridge for the start of the 2015 Ashes test when we agreed that we wouldn't have a drink until England took a wicket. It took three balls. How many were Australia all out for that morning? (we struggled to keep up!)

6. At the 1981 FA Cup Final between Tottenham Hotspur and Manchester City. Who scored for both teams in the 1-1 draw?

7. When Ben Stokes made his maiden test century in a losing cause on the 2013-14 Ashes tour. At which ground?

8. At the 2012 Welsh Grand National (run in January 2013 after a postponement) when which horse, owned by rugby players Mike Tindall, James Simpson-Daniel and Nicky Robinson, was the winner?

9. My first trip to Wembley was for the 1979 rugby league Challenge Cup final, played between clubs whose home grounds were at that time called Naughton Park and Belle Vue. Who were the teams?

10. In 2013 I was team manager of Malvern RFC U17s and was summoned together with the coaches on a club disciplinary matter, as we were in trouble for allowing an U15 player to be among our replacements in one game when we were short, and for letting him to play for the last ten minutes. We didn't worry unduly as his dad was one of the coaches and, from the player's size and demeanour, nobody would have guessed he was two years younger. Five years later I was delighted to be at Twickenham to see the same player make his full England debut, again off the bench, at the age of 19 against Japan. Who was the player?

* After I had written this question, Chris asked Harry Redknapp what he remembered of the game, and the response was 'we got absolutely battered!'. That would do it, thanks Harry.

11. LIKE FATHER LIKE SON

1. Which father and son have kept goal for the Danish international team and in club matches have both kept a clean sheet in a 9-0 win?

2. Which father, who won 23 rugby union caps between 1972 and 1980, had two sons who emulated him in winning international caps for Wales?

3. Which current National Hunt racehorse trainer has a father who won an Olympic individual show jumping gold medal in 2016?

4. Which footballer represented both Chelsea and Barcelona, and remarkably made his international debut coming on as a substitute for his father?

5. Which jockey won 13 Italian riding championships, and has a son who has won over 500 Group races?

6. Which two footballers were colleagues at the same London club between 1967 and 1972, and have sons who both became England internationals? The sons are also cousins.

7. Which father and son opposed each other in Six Nations internationals in 2020, with the father being coach of his son's opponents? Ironically they once played for the same professional club.

8. Which father and son, one "Old" and the other "Young", each won four Open golf championships?

9. Which father and son have both been British and Commonwealth heavyweight boxing champions?

10. Who is the only footballer to be knighted whilst still playing, and is the oldest player to play top-flight English football, and had a son who won junior Wimbledon?

12. WEIGHTS AND MEASURES

1. What is made of vulcanised rubber, is black, one inch thick, three inches in diameter, and weighs between 5½ and 6 ounces?

2. Which sport introduced a minimum height requirement of 173cm in 1994, but has no weight requirements or classification?

3. In pitch terms, what did 25 become in 1977, even though the nearest equivalent would have actually been one more?

4. Who in 1979 caused controversy by employing aluminium rather than wood because, as he pointed out, there was nothing in the Laws at that time to say that he couldn't?

5. Which sport is played on the biggest marked out pitch?

6. How long, in feet, is a standard UK full sized snooker table?

7. Mohammad Irfan, the current Pakistani fast bowler, is the tallest player ever to have played international cricket. To the nearest inch, how tall is he?

8. What is the maximum number of clubs a golfer is allowed in his bag?

9. The official rules of which sport state that the ball shall be spherical, with a diameter of 40mm and weigh 2.7g?

10. What weight do all colts carry in the Epsom Derby?

13. FIRST IMPRESSIONS

1. Who made a stunning start to his participation in the Tour de France when he not only claimed the general classification, but also the points and mountain classifications, the only man ever to do so?

2. Whose win at the 2003 Open Golf championship was not just his first appearance at the Open, but his first ever at any Major? He was a 300-1 outsider before the start.

3. Who made his Real Madrid debut in September 2005, over a year after signing from Newcastle United because of injury, scored a spectacular own goal after 25 minutes, got booked, and then sent off for a second bookable offence?

4. More notably, who scored on his debuts for Chelsea, AC Milan, Tottenham Hotspur, West Ham and England?

5. Which Welshman was a rank outsider on his world championship debut at the Crucible in 1979, but won the final against Dennis Taylor?

6. Andy Ganteaume of the West Indies and New Zealander Rodney Redmond share what individual cricketing record?

7. Which rugby player, formerly a bricklayer, scored a hat-trick of tries on his England debut against Romania in 1989, and went on to play 65 times for his country and eight times for the British Lions?

8. Which 23-year-old darts player from Ipswich turned up for his first world championship in 1983 as a virtual unknown, but beat Jocky Wilson and John Lowe before defeating Eric Bristow 6-5 in one of the greatest finals in darts history?

9. Four sports will make their debut at the Tokyo Olympics (as opposed to sports returning after an absence). Karate and Skateboarding are two, name either of the others?

10. Which Australian had match figures of 16 for 137 on his Test debut at Lord's in 1972, the fourth best Test bowling figures of all time?

14. GENUINE ALL-ROUNDERS

1. Which British tennis player won three consecutive Wimbledon Men's Singles titles between 1934 and 1936 but, prior to this, had been world table tennis champion in 1929?

2. Who competed for the US in four Olympics, winning a 110m hurdle gold medal in 1968, but then in 1980 competed in the Winter Olympics as a member of the US bobsleigh team?

3. Which former England international rugby union player has in early 2020 signed a "reserve / future" contract with the Buffalo Bills?

4. Who in 1964 gained an FA Cup final winners' medal, a county cricket championship winners' medal, and topped the first-class bowling averages?

5. Who in 1960 came within one shot of qualifying for the British Olympic clay pigeon shooting team in Rome, before going on to win 27 Formula 1 races?

6. Who retired from tennis in 1893, having won five Wimbledon Ladies' titles, played hockey for England, became the British amateur golf champion and then competed at archery in the 1908 Olympics?

7. Who won four caps at Under 21 football for England in 1999, and became British lightweight boxing champion in 2012?

8. Who won a middleweight boxing gold medal at the 1908 Olympics, then captained England at cricket on 18 occasions between 1911 and 1921, and also played for England in an amateur football international?

9. Which American is the only man to win gold medals at both the Summer Olympics (boxing in 1920), and the Winter Olympics (four-man bobsleigh in 1932)?

10. Which goalkeeper retired from football in 2019, holding the record for the most clean sheets in English Premier League history, and now plays semi-professional ice hockey for Guildford Phoenix?

15. FOR THOSE WATCHING IN BLACK AND WHITE

1. What sport uses ONLY red, black, blue and yellow balls?

2. Gold is the colour at the centre of an archery target, but what colour are the two outer rings?

3. According to its constitution (having been founded in 1866), which club's colours are maroon, pale blue, sage green, black and gold?

4. In which classification of the Tour de France does the leader wear a polka dot jersey?

5. What colours are always worn by a greyhound coming out of trap six?

6. What colour is the zero on a roulette wheel?

7. What colour appears in the name of a horse that has won three post-war Grand Nationals?

8. Who was the 2019 wearer of the Green Jacket?

9. What colour of shirts are worn by the most southerly football league club in England?

10. What sport uses the "double yellow" ball as the official ball for all national and international tournaments?

16. GIANT KILLERS AND UNDERDOGS

1. In which city did USA defeat England 1-0 in a World Cup Finals group match in 1950?

2. Which Scotsman came from 10 shots behind at the start of the final round to win the 1999 Open Championship?

3. Who are the only non-Test cricket nation to reach a one day World Cup semi-final?

4. Who won the 2001 Men's Singles title at Wimbledon as a wild card entry, defeating Pat Rafter in the final?

5. Who shot to overnight stardom by defeating reigning champion Steve Davies 10-1 in the first round of the 1982 World Snooker Championships?

6. What was the last horse to win the Cheltenham Gold Cup at odds of 100-1?

7. Who won the 2004 European Football Championship, having been priced at 150-1 by the bookmakers prior to the tournament?

8. Who in 1973 became the first first-class county to lose to a minor county in cricket's Gillette Cup, when Durham (still a minor county then) beat them by five wickets?

9. Who was the 42-1 underdog who beat Mike Tyson to win the world heavyweight title and cause what is acknowledged as the biggest upset in boxing history?

10. Michael Edwards, a real underdog, finished stone last in his two events at the 1988 Winter Olympics, but by what name was he better known (a film of the same name was released in 2016)?

17. AUSSIE RULES

1. Which Australian woman was the first of only three swimmers to have won the same event at three consecutive Olympic games; and held the 100 metre freestyle world record for 15 years?

2. Which Australian cricketer was disappointingly bowled second ball for nought by Eric Hollies in his final Test match, and thus found his Test average lowered to below 100 (it ended at 99.94)?

3. Which Australian runner, now chairman of one of the largest iron ore mining companies in the world, never lost a 1,500 metre or one mile race between 1957 and 1961?

4. Which champion racehorse, often referred to as "Australia's Wonder Horse", won 37 of his 51 races, and has a life-sized bronze statue at Flemington racecourse?

5. Which Australian racing driver was Formula 1 world champion in 1959, 1960 and 1966, and now has a Formula 1 racing team running cars under his name?

6. Which Australian rugby league player, who retired in 1994, is still the top points scorer in State of Origin football; and is now the head coach of the Australian national team?

7. Which Australian speedway rider born in Bristol won the world championships in 2004, 2006 and 2009, retired in 2012 – but was announced as coming out of retirement to ride for Ipswich Witches in 2020?

8. Which female Australian tennis player won a record number of 64 major tennis titles, and is currently a Christian minister in Perth?

9. Which Australian goalkeeper won a record 109 International caps for his country, and also made 562 league appearances for English clubs?

10. Which Australian golfer won the Open Golf title five times between 1954 and 1966, and designed over a hundred golf courses in Australia and around the world?

18. PASSPORT CONTROL

Who was born in:

1. Louisville, Kentucky - in 1942, and changed his name in 1964?

2. Sri Lanka, played seven Test matches for Australia in 1989, and has coached the Sri Lanka, Bangladesh, Pakistan and Zimbabwe national teams?

3. Singapore - played football 77 times for England between 1980 and 1990 and, after leaving his first club, also enjoyed success – playing and managing – in Scotland?

4. Dayton, Ohio - and is a regular member of the current England rugby union squad?

5. Ghent, Belgium - to an Australian father and British mother, and had a stellar year in 2012?

6. Montreal - and caused controversy when he switched his allegiance to Britain in 1995?

7. Johannesburg – and representing Great Britain won the gold in the 2016 Olympic golf competition, along the way becoming the first golfer to make a hole-in-one at the Olympics?

8. Mogadishu, Somalia - moved to Britain at the age of 8 and was BBC Sports Personality of the Year in 2017?

9. Milan - and captained England at cricket?

10. Guernsey - spent his entire professional club career with one south coast football team, and won eight caps for England?

19. TAKE YOUR PARTNERS

1. What were the names of "The Woodies", one of the most successful pairings in tennis history, who won 61 ATP doubles tournaments, including 11 Grand Slam titles?

2. Which Russian skater won ten successive world pairs championships between 1969 and 1978, and three successive Olympic gold medals in partnership with either Alexei Ulanov or Alexander Rodnina?

3. Nick Faldo won six golf Majors in his career, but who was his caddie for some 14 years?

4. Who were the two former international footballers who presented a Saturday ITV football programme at lunchtime, prior to the afternoon's games? The show ran from 1985 to1992, when ITV lost the rights to broadcast top tier English matches to Sky?

5. Who were the driver and the brakeman in the British bobsleigh that won the gold medal in the two-man event at the 1964 Winter Olympics in Innsbruck?

6. Which two players made up the legendary Real Madrid striking partnership, with the Hungarian scoring 157 goals in his eight seasons, and the Argentinian scoring 216 in his eleven seasons?

7. Who made up the most successful opening partnership in Test cricket history, sharing 16 century stands with four over 200, and amassing 6,482 runs altogether?

8. Which two rowers won gold medals in the coxless pairs at both the Barcelona and Atlanta Olympics?

9. Which Irish horse and jockey dominated British jump racing in the early/mid 1960's, winning three consecutive Cheltenham Gold Cups?

10. Which member of an Olympic medal winning duo said of their relationship "I sometimes think it's like a marriage really, apart from he fact that we spend the nights separately"?

20. HOLY ORDERS

1. Which rugby player, whose father was at one time Britain's no.1 squash player, was the first number eight to score four tries for England in an international and retired in 2016 having made a record 281 appearances for Harlequins?

2. Which Australian all-rounder is a T20 specialist and holds the record for the highest T20 score for a player batting at no.5 (129) and at no.6 (113*)?

3. Who in 1787 acquired seven acres of land off Dorset Square, London and so bought his first cricket ground, then briefly bought a second ground before buying his third ground in St John's Wood in 1814?

4. Who scored 383 goals for Everton in 433 appearances, including a record 60 league goals in the 1927-1928 season and has a statue outside Goodison Park?

5. Which baseball team have won eleven World Series championships, more than any other MLB team?

6. Who is the current chairman and part-owner of Crystal Palace?

7. The Church's stand was opened in 2002 at which premiership rugby ground?

8. Which current Manchester City footballer initially chose to wear the number 33 on his shirt in tribute to the age at which Jesus Christ is believed to have been crucified?

9. Who made his maiden test hundred in the third Test at Port Elizabeth in January 2020?

10. Which darts player won the world championship in 2018 on his debut in the competition and in doing so became the only player to win, having survived match darts in two earlier games?

21. FACE THE MUSIC

1. On 3 June 2016 at his concert in Berkeley, California, Paul Simon stopped singing halfway through his song "The Boxer" to break the news to the audience that who had passed away?

2. What was the title of the hit song recorded by Chas and Dave in 1986, with backing vocalists known as "The Matchroom Mob"?

3. Tranmere Rovers supporters Half Man Half Biscuit had a plaintive song about playing Subutteo as a boy. Which team's playing kit did they covet?

4. Which former Glamorgan and England cricketer featured in the song "Mr Carbohydrate" by the Manic Street Preachers?

5. During the 2003 Rugby World Cup in Australia, which Welshman totally sold out a concert at the Sydney Opera House?

6. Survivor's "Eye of the Tiger" is very much associated with Sylvester Stallone, but which boxer covered it in 1995, his championship year, reaching number 28 in the charts?

7. In the song "Where Do You Go To (My Lovely)", recorded by Peter Sarstedt, what was it that the Aga Khan sent her for Christmas?

8. The Liverpool anthem "You'll never walk alone" gained its popularity after which group released the song in 1963?

9. Which wrestler, christened Terry Gene Bollea, used the song "Real American" as his entrance theme song?

10. Billy Bragg's song "God's footballer" refers to which former Wolves player (and brother of a Tottenham and England full back) who retired from the game in 1970 after becoming a Jehovah's Witness? Wolves retained his contract for over ten years in case he ever changed his mind.

22. CHRISTIAN NAMES AS SURNAMES

1. Which fly half gained 70 England caps prior to becoming director of elite rugby at the RFU, and is currently chief executive of Sussex CCC?

2. Which boxer, himself a world heavyweight champion, was the only man to take Rocky Marciano the distance over 15 rounds, and was a neighbour and friend of Muhammad Ali when they both lived on 85th Street in Chicago?

3. Which flamboyant darts player, often making his way to the stage bedecked in jewellery and wearing a crown, lives in his own self-built mansion with the hall actually named after him, and the rooms designed and set out to look like a dartboard?

4. Who represented New Zealand at rugby league, still holds the record of kicking most goals in a Super League season with 178 for Bradford Bulls in 2001, but later represented England at rugby union?

5. Who at the Oval in 1994 was so incensed by being hit on the head by a bouncer from Fanie de Villiers that he responded by taking 9-57 in the South African innings, the best bowling analysis in twentieth century cricket by an England fast bowler?

6. Which Welsh conditional jockey rode Happy Diva to win the Bet Victor Gold Cup at Cheltenham in November 2019?

7. Which centre half made 357 appearances for Tottenham Hotspur and won 23 caps for England, prior to his career being ended with a double fracture of his tibia and fibula?

8. Who has born in Jamaica in 1955 and was eleven times English table tennis champion?

9. Golfer Rickie Fowler wore plus fours and argyle socks at the 2014 US Open at the Pinehurst Resort as a tribute to which golfer who had won his last Major championship at that same venue, only a short time before he died in a plane crash?

10. Which female jockey rode over 100 winners in the calendar year 2017, becoming only the second female jockey to do so?

23. SURNAMES AS CHRISTIAN NAMES

The ten surnames in the answers to the previous round are the Christian names in the ten answers to this round, but not in the same order.

1. Which golfer won the 2009 Open Championship at Turnberry, defeating Tom Watson in a play off?

2. Which West Indian fast bowler had a Test bowling average of 20.94, the best average of anyone who has taken more than 200 Test wickets? Sadly, he died at the early age of 41, and his funeral in Barbados was led by the Rev Wes Hall.

3. Which former world heavyweight champion has been married five times with ten children – five sons and five daughters – with the sons all being named George Edward? He said on CBN:
"When you've been hit as many times as I have, you're not going to remember names anymore"

4. Which national hunt jockey with the nickname "Lensio", due to his short sightedness, retired in 2018 having ridden more than 1,000 winners?

5. Which footballer is the youngest player to take part in a World Cup, and the youngest player to score in a League Cup Final and an FA Cup Final?

6. Will Carling and Jeremy Guscott made a record 44 appearances as an international rugby centre partnership until it was broken by Brian O'Driscoll and which other player?

7. Which Australian tennis player was the third man in the Open era, after Rod Laver and Stefan Edberg, to have reached the semi-finals (or better) of every Grand Slam tournament in both singles and doubles?

8. Who was born Angelo Siciliano in New York in 1893, but changed his name in 1922, and set up a business under his new name marketing a fitness programme for the "97-pound weakling", which is still operating today?

9. Which famous musician embarrassingly missed his cue and fell out of time with his pre-recorded vocals and backing track, as he was about to sing the closing number at Danny Boyle's 2012 Olympic opening ceremony?

10. Which climber, the son of an ABA heavyweight boxing champion, was the first mountaineer to ascend the south west face of Mount Everest in 1975?

24. MAMMA MIA

1. Who is the third most capped international rugby union player of all time? His first wife was originally Miss France and then became Miss Europe in 2006.

2. Which former Formula 1 motor racing world champion was killed at Monza, on the same day of the month as his father had died in an accident in the French Grand Prix in 1925?

3. Who played football 32 times for Italy; then managed Milan, Real Madrid, Roma and Juventus, before being appointed manager of England in 2007?

4. Who won five out of five points when Europe won the 2018 Ryder Cup?

5. Which skier, nicknamed "La Bamba", won three Olympic golds and two world championships, and brought the Olympic flame into the stadium in Turin at the 2006 Winter Olympics opening ceremony?

6. Which athlete originally competed for Great Britain before representing Italy in the long jump, twice winning the world championships?

7. Which goalkeeper gained 176 Italian international football caps, and has made over 1,000 professional career appearances, over 500 of them for Juventus?

8. Which 40-year old rider has competed in over 400 motor cycling Grand Prix, including nine world championship wins, and is reputedly one of the highest ever earning sporting superstars, despite persistent enquiries from the Italian tax authorities?

9. Which racing team is the oldest and most successful in Formula 1 history, with a record 16 constructors' championships and 15 driving championships?

10. Which Italian, nicknamed "The Ambling Alp" because of his huge size, was world heavyweight boxing champion, appeared in many films, and then won 120 straight wrestling matches before suffering his first defeat?

25. ANOTHER DOOR OPENS

1. Which former British Lion went on to become chief executive of Heinz?

2. Who was a member of France's synchronised swimming team as a teenager and until 2019 was the managing director of the International Monetary Fund?

3. Which member of England's 1966 World Cup winning team became an undertaker after hanging up his boots?

4. Which tennis player won ten Grand Slam titles, but is probably better known now from his name's appearance on the casual shirt brand he created, which features a green crocodile logo?

5. Who was a sufficiently accomplished college football player that, when he left, the University of Michigan retired his number 48 jersey, although he was rather better known for becoming President of the United States?

6. Which three-time world heavyweight champion went on to become a member of the Ukrainian parliament and is now mayor of Kiev?

7. Who played 22 Test matches for England in the 50s and 60s, and later became Bishop of Liverpool?

8. Which English World Cup winning rugby player set up a clothing brand, which uses the nickname from his playing days?

9. Who held the British record for the 100 metres from 1967 to 1974, and was the leader of the Liberal Democrats from March 2006 until October 2007?

10. Which English footballer gave up a new career managing a carp lake in France to return to football as Charlton Athletic's manager in 2018?

26. ROGUES AND VILLAINS

1. Eight members of which baseball team were accused of throwing the 1919 World Series against the Cincinnati Reds in exchange for cash, an event dramatised in the 1988 film "Eight men out"?

2. Who was the coach banned for three years after his involvement in the "Bloodgate" affair?

3. Which former American footballer was originally acquitted of the murder of his former wife, Nicole Brown, and her friend Ron Goldman, but thirteen years later was then jailed for 33 years for the offence?

4. Which multiple champion flat jockey and winner of thirty English Classics was jailed for three years for tax evasion?

5. Who in 2012 was named the ringleader of "the most sophisticated, professionalised and successful doping programme that sport has ever seen"?

6. Which figure skater was banned for life in 1994, after admitting that she had been involved in a vicious attack on American rival Nancy Kerrigan?

7. Diego Maradona's infamous "hand of God" goal was scored against which goalkeeper?

8. Which Test cricketer was arrested at Gatwick Airport in 2008, on suspicion of smuggling cocaine, and was jailed for 13 years?

9. Boris Onishchenko was disqualified for cheating at which sport at the 1976 Olympics?

10. Which Test cricket captain, later to die in an air-crash, was banned for life in 2000, after it was revealed that a conversation had taken place between him and bookmaker Sanjay Chawla?

27. JOB DESCRIPTIONS

1. Who in 1964 was signed by Coventry City manager, Jimmy Hill, for what was then a world record fee for a goalkeeper of £35,000?

2. Who was beaten in the 1979 Wimbledon final by Bjorn Borg, and once had his rapid left-handed serve clocked at 153 mph?

3. Which boxer lost to Muhammad Ali in 1966, and was the first boxer to twice win BBC Sports Personality of the Year?

4. Which Indian Test cricketer became a popular talisman of Lancashire when they were the undisputed kings of one day cricket in the 1970's?

5. Which American jockey retired in 1990, having ridden an astonishing 8,833 winners?

6. Who scored over 100 goals in both the English and Scottish leagues, and was the first professional footballer to play for England without having previously played in the English football league?

7. Who stood 7' 1" tall, and is the only player to score 100 points in a single NBA game; and off the field remained a lifelong bachelor, becoming notorious for his claim of having had sexual relations with as many as 20,000 women?

8. Which batsman, born in Gloucester, is England's most capped player, and has scored a record 33 Test centuries for England?

9. Which darts player, nicknamed "The Artist", is renowned his many arguments and run-ins with Phil Taylor?

10. Which boxer lost his world title in "The Rumble in The Jungle" in 1974?

28. TEN TO ONE

This is an easy round because you know the answers before you start. The answers are the numbers one to ten. You just have to work out the order and you can use each answer only once!

1. How many times did Jack Nicklaus win the US Masters?

2. How many goals did Paul Gascoigne score in his England career?

3. In crown green bowls, how many bowls does each player have?

4. How many times have Glamorgan won the county cricket championship?

5. How many times did Lester Piggott win the Epsom Derby?

6. How many gold medals did Great Britain win at the Atlanta Olympics in 1996?

7. Muhammad Ali had 61 professional fights - how many did he lose?

8. Up to and including the 2019 rugby World Cup semi-final, how many times have England beaten the All Blacks?

9. How many Olympic medals, of all colours, did Rebecca Adlington win?

10. How many individual stage wins in the Tour de France does Chris Froome have?

29. CASH IS KING

1. Which centre-forward was transferred from Newcastle United to Arsenal in 1976, for the unusual fee of £333,333.34?

2. Which ground has been sponsored by AMP, Fosters and Brit Insurance prior to its current naming rights deal?

3. Which beer brand was the first sponsor to appear on the All Blacks' jersey, in 1994?

4. Who won the first Wimbledon Men's Singles of the "Open Era" in tennis, ie when Grand Slam tournaments agreed to allow professional players to compete with amateurs?

5. Which 2011 film starring Brad Pitt portrayed the Oakland Athletics baseball team's 2002 season, and their attempt to build a team of undervalued talent through the use of sophisticated statistics?

6. Coolmore Stud in Ireland publishes its fees for the 'services' of its various stallions. For 2020, which is the only horse whose stud fee is not actually quoted, but is listed as 'Private'?

7. Who in 1988 won the US Open and also became the first golfer to win $1million in a season on the PGA Tour?

8. Which firm became the first sponsors of the FA Cup in 1994?

9. Which sport in the UK has received the most funding for the Tokyo Olympics?

10. Tennis player Ilie Nastase became the first professional sportsperson to be sponsored by which company?

30. WHERE IN THE COUNTRY

1. What is the most northerly full-time professional football team in the UK?

2. Which racecourse is situated on the top of Haldon Hill?

3. In which county would you compete in the annual Three Peaks Race, climbing Ingleborough, Pen-y-ghent and Whernside?

4. Which Welsh Ryder Cup player learned to play the game at Llanmynech golf course? Fifteen of its holes are In Wales and the other three are in England, and at the 4th hole you actually drive off in Wales and putt out on English soil – a real dilemma as we come out of "lockdown"!

5. At an altitude of 551 feet above sea level, which is the highest of all the 92 Football League grounds?

6. On what stretch of water does the Cowes Week Regatta take place?

7. On what sands was the legendary racehorse Red Rum trained?

8. Which Japanese climber was the first woman to ascend the highest peak on each of the seven continents, including her being the first woman to reach the summit of Everest in 1975?

9. Where exactly was the bowling green on which Sir Francis Drake was reportedly playing when the Spanish Armada was first sighted?

10. The first horse race known as the Cheltenham Gold Cup took place in July 1819. It was a flat race over three miles, on top of which hill?

31. LESSONS FROM HISTORY AND LITERATURE

1. Who was reputedly watching a game of tennis at the Palace of Whitehall when she was arrested for high treason and sent to the Tower of London?

2. Fever Pitch: A Fan's Life is a book by Nick Hornby relating the author's beloved relationship with which football club?

3. The quote from Kipling's poem: "If you can meet with triumph and disaster, and treat those two impostors just the same" appears at which sporting venue, above the door as the competitors leave their changing room to go and play?

4. In which novel does Mr Jingle provide a commentary on a cricket match between All Muggleton and Dingley Dell?

5. In a scene from Antony and Cleopatra what sport does Cleopatra play with Charmian the eunuch, giving her plenty of opportunity to tease him about his disability?

6. "I see you stand like greyhounds in the slips straining upon the start, the game's afoot". Which king, according to Shakespeare, offered these words?

7. Which crime writer, born in Scotland in 1859, played ten first-class cricket matches for MCC, but took only one wicket, that of WG Grace?

8. Which famous Olympian, as competitor and administrator, was named after a character from Shakespeare's "The Tempest"? He has a sister called Miranda!

9. "There's a breathless hush in the Close tonight [?] to make and the match to win". Fill in the brackets with the number of runs were needed to win this game in the famous poem Vitai Lampada by Sir Henry Newbolt?

10. What sporting gift did the French Dauphin send to King Henry V?

32. THE AMERICAN DREAM

1. Which athlete won a gold medal at the 1968 Olympics, at the same time revolutionising the high jump event with his very own "back first" technique?

2. Who is the most decorated Olympian, of all time, with a total of 28 medals, including 23 golds?

3. Which tennis player had a "career golden slam" with victories in all four Grand Slam tournaments plus an Olympic gold medal, and was first married to Brooke Shields and then to Steffi Graf?

4. Which basketball player in 1999 was named by ESPN as "the greatest athlete of the 20th century"?

5. Who set a world long jump record at the Mexico City Olympics in 1968 that stood for almost 28 years?

6. Which soccer player won both the Golden Boot and Golden Ball awards at the 2019 FIFA Women's World Cup in France?

7. Which American won the Formula 1 world championship in 1978?

8. Which American golfer finished first, second and third in three of the four Major golf tournaments in 2019?

9. Which American scholar at Oxford was selected to play in the University Rugby match within three months of ever playing a game of rugby, and created rugby history by inventing the torpedo pass from the line out?

10. Which American goalkeeper holds the record for the most consecutive Premier League appearances (310)?

33. TOWNS AND CITIES IN THE UK

1. Which British sprinter was the 100 metre Olympic champion in 1980?

2. Which leg spinner played in 15 Test cricket matches for England between 1992 and 2000?

3. Who was the first person to sail single-handedly around the world by the clipper route in his ketch Gipsy Moth IV?

4. Who was the former Spurs full back who suddenly went into cardiac arrest at the age of 49, whilst managing Leyton Orient?

5. Which international rugby player moved from his native Wales to play for an English premiership club in 2018?

6. Which British athlete, who usually ran in distinctive red socks, set a world record for the 10,000 metres in 1973?

7. Which promising young Worcestershire cricketer lost his right arm below the elbow at Salonica in 1917, but after the war became the world's leading umpire, standing in Test matches for 31 years?

8. Who was the legendary cornerman and trainer who worked with the likes of Muhammad Ali, Sugar Ray Leonard, George Foreman and Jose Napoles?

9. Who rode the 100-1 outsider Foinavon to win the 1967 Grand National?

10. Who was the head coach of the England rugby union team from 2011 to 2015?

34. OVER THE HILLS AND FAR AWAY

1. The Four Hills ski jumping competition is held annually around New Year over four venues, in which two countries?

2. Which British athlete won the world heptathlon championships on three occasions, and during her career set British records for the 100m hurdles and high jump?

3. The Hillsborough stadium disaster occurred in April 1989, but who were Liverpool's scheduled opponents on that day?

4. Which climb, now rated the most popular in the world by Strava website, featured in both the men's and women's road races at the 2012 Olympics?

5. Graham and Damon Hill have both won the world Formula 1 Drivers' Championship, but who are the only other father and son to do so?

6. Which country first introduced the sport of ski jumping?

7. Which two unrelated England rugby union players share the same christian and surnames, and both coincidentally attended Bishops Wordsworth School and played for Salisbury RFC?

8. The London to Sydney Air Race, last held in 2001, started from which airfield?

9. Coopers Hill in Gloucestershire holds an annual race every Spring Bank Holiday when the contestants chase what down the precipitous hill?

10. Which English marathon runner, a Commonwealth Games and European gold medallist, did not miss a day's running between 20 December 1964 and 30 January 2017, a total of 52 years and 39 days? With a minimum one mile per day, he logged a total mileage of over 150,000 miles!

35. BROTHERLY LOVE

1. Which current England rugby international has five brothers who have all played senior international rugby?

2. Who were the brothers who finished first and second in the 2016 Olympic triathlon?

3. Who were the twins who won the Wimbledon Men's Doubles' titles in 2006, 2011 and 2013?

4. Which Australian cricketer is the brother of the men's high jump gold medallist at the 2018 Commonwealth games?

5. Which three brothers have regularly played rugby together for Sale Sharks in 2019-2020 season?

6. Who were the last brothers, prior to Tom and Sam Curran, to play international cricket together for England?

7. Which brothers gained 179 international football caps between them (the one a record 112 caps, the other 67 caps) playing for Holland?

8. Which brothers played football together in the 1966 World Cup final?

9. Who are the only brothers in history to both win a Formula 1 Grand Prix, and on five occasions to finish first and second in the same Grand Prix?

10. Which brothers have combined for over 90,000 passing yards and 647 touchdown passes, and have both won Super Bowls and been the game's MVP?

36. THE NUMBERS BOARD

1. What is the highest score you can make with your last three arrows to win a game of darts?

2. How many completed miles does an athlete run in the Olympic marathon?

3. How many competitors take part in the annual Oxford v Cambridge Boat Race?

4. What is the highest number of wickets taken by an individual bowler in a Test match?

5. How many completed games did Djokovic and Federer play in the fifth set of 2019's Wimbledon Men's Final before going to the tie-break decider?

6. How many teams started the 2019-20 season in the English Football League, ie the three divisions below the Premier League?

7. How many minutes from the first bell to the last in a World Heavyweight Championship boxing bout?

8. What is the maximum number by which the count cannot be exceeded in a game of cribbage?

9. How many fences does a horse jump before winning the Grand National?

10. To mark England's 1000th international football match in October 2019 the players started wearing legacy numbers on their shirts, to mark how many players had received England caps. Chelsea's Fikayo Tomori is the latest player in the list, but what is his number?

37. IT'S A DOG'S LIFE

1. Which greyhound was brought to England in 1929 by an Irish priest, Father Brophy, and became an icon in the sport and once won 19 races in a row including two English Derbies?

2. What was the name of the dog invited to the celebration banquet for England winning the 1966 World Cup, because he had come across the World Cup trophy wrapped in a newspaper in a South London street after it had been stolen?

3. Which centre forward played 223 games for Burnley between 1957 and 1964 gaining three England caps?

4. What is the oldest rowing race in the world, taking place on the Thames over 4 miles 5 furlongs and held every year since 1715?

5. What is the name of the pub in Tinsley Green which hosts the annual world marbles championships?

6. Which England wicket keeper made his highest Test score of 128* against Australia at Old Trafford in 1989 in an epic lost-cause six hour innings, which was also his maiden century in all forms of cricket?

7. The Greyhound Derby ceased to be run at Wimbledon Stadium in 2016 and then moved to a new track built on the in-field of which racecourse? The course closed in 2018.

8. Davey Boy Smith defeated his real-life brother-in-law, Bret Hart, in a WWF heavyweight championship fight at Wembley Stadium in front of 82,000 spectators in 1992. Under what other name did he wrestle?

9. O'Neil Gordon Smith was a talented West Indian cricketer who made a century on his debut against Australia followed by a pair in the next Test. Sadly he died at the early age of 26 from injuries sustained in a car crash when he was heading to a charity match with Gary Sobers. By what name was he commonly known?

10. The Kennels is the central clubhouse for all of which estate's sporting members, be it horseracing, golf, motorsport, aviation or health club enthusiasts?

38. THE SMITHS

1. Who in 1971 shamelessly gave a "V" sign to the judges, following a near perfect round which won him the British show jumping Derby at Hickstead?

2. Which gymnast won individual medals on the pommel horse at the 2008, 2012 and 2016 Olympic Games, and also won the 2012 series of Strictly Come Dancing?

3. Which American athlete won the men's 200m gold medal at the 1968 Olympics, but made headline news with his black power salute with John Carlos, atop the medal podium?

4. Who won just one Test cap for England, and founded the Hollywood Cricket Club in 1932 while he was starring in films alongside such luminaries as Clark Gable, Greta Garbo, Laurence Olivier and Vivien Leigh?

5. Who is England cricket's national selector, whose book "On and Off the Field" was short listed for the William Hill Sports Book of the Year in 2004?

6. Which American jockey rode the American horse Jay Trump to victory in the 1965 Grand National?

7. What are the Christian names of the four Smith boxing brothers from Liverpool, who have all been British champions?

8. Which TCCB chief executive (from 1986 to 1996) kept wicket for both Warwickshire and England, but also, against Essex in 1965, achieved the extraordinary feat of taking a hat-trick as a bowler in a match for which he was selected as a wicket keeper?

9. Who was the referee who abandoned the Manchester derby in 1974 with eight minutes remaining, and the United fans spilling onto the pitch with United losing 1-0, and so virtually doomed to relegation? (other results meant that United would be relegated anyway, hence the final abandonment)

10. And to finish, who is the narrator and protagonist in Alan Sillitoe's "The Loneliness of the Long-Distance Runner"?

39. CAPTAIN MARVELS

1. Which All Black is currently the most capped Test rugby player of all time, and captained the team in 110 of his 148 Tests?

2. Which captain was the mastermind behind the infamous bodyline tactic that characterised the Ashes in Australia in 1932-1933?

3. Which two footballers have each captained the England football team on a record 90 occasions?

4. Who captained the GB rugby league team to victory over Australia in 1958, despite breaking his arm just four minutes into the game?

5. Thomas Bjorn and Jim Furyk, the respective European and American Ryder Cup captains in 2008, recreated an iconic moment in history by hitting golf balls off the top of where, 41 years after the legendary Arnold Palmer had been the first and only person to do so?

6. Who played a record 17 times for the British Lions and was captain on their most successful tour ever – a 3-0 series defeat of South Africa in 1974?

7. Who captained England at the 2018 FIFA World Cup?

8. Who were the very first two captains on A Question of Sport, when it was first broadcast in 1970?

9. Which other Question of Sport captain once mistook Princess Anne for a male jockey in a picture round?

10. Which horse won the Cheltenham Gold Cup in 1974 as a novice, and then won the King George VI Chase in both 1974 and 1975?

40. COMPASS POINTS

1. Who is the second highest all time try scorer for Wales in rugby union behind Shane Williams?

2. What word describes the group of sports that require navigational skills using a map and compass to navigate from point to point in diverse and unfamiliar terrain?

3. Which football club, originally known as Thomas Ironworks FC, moved in 2016 from their former home, the Boleyn Ground, to the London Stadium?

4. The Southern Sydney Rabbitohs were regular wooden spoonists in the National Rugby League until 2006, when which actor bought a 50% share in the club and immediately transformed their results?

5. What high jumping technique was preceded by the "scissors" and succeeded by the "straddle" techniques?

6. Which current Hampshire cricketer was a schoolboy prodigy and the youngest cricketer for 60 years to appear at Lord's in the Eton v Harrow match?

7. Which footballer sued Newcastle United in 1963 over the player registration rules and won a court case which proved a landmark in improving players' freedom to move between clubs?

8. Which broadcaster was recommended to the BBC by C B Fry in 1947, making his name as a tennis and cricket commentator as well as presenting such programmes such as Come Dancing and What's My Line?

9. A point-to-point is a localised form of horseracing for hunting horses and amateur jockeys that began in 1752 when the riders would race across country from one point to another. What were these specific "points" in those days?

10. Who was the Essex left arm spinner who took over 1,000 first class wickets and was regarded as the most hilarious practical joker on the professional cricket circuit?

41. THE SILVER SCREEN

1. The film Million Dollar Baby starring Clint Eastwood is themed around which sport?

2. What was the title of the film released in 1993, that is loosely based on the true story of the Jamaican team's debut in competition at the 1988 Winter Olympics?

3. A young Elizabeth Taylor plays Velvet Brown in the film National Velvet. What is the name of the horse on which she wins the Grand National?

4. Which British historical drama film tells the fact-based story of two athletes taking part in the 1924 Olympics?

5. Pele and Bobby Moore were among the more illustrious names to appear in the film Escape to Victory, but which English club provided both the goalkeepers for the two teams – Allies and Germans – despite the fact that one of the players was actually a winger?

6. In what film does "Fast Eddie" Felson take on the legendary "Minnesota Fats"?

7. This Sporting Life, starring Richard Harris and Rachel Roberts, centres on which particular sport?

8. In which Bond film did India's leading tennis player, Vijay Amritraj, play Bond's MI6 ally in India?

9. In what film does Mickey Rourke play Randy "The Ram" Robinson?

10. In what film did James Caan play for Houston in a futuristic story of a life and death sport?

42. HOT STREAKS

1. Which swimmer, later known for playing Tarzan in films, never lost a competitive race during his entire amateur career, including winning three Olympic gold medals?

2. Which squash player had a remarkable 555 consecutive wins from 1981 to 1986?

3. Which darts player won eight consecutive PDC World Darts titles from 1995 to 2002?

4. Which jockey rode twelve consecutive winners over three days in October 1933?

5. The America's Cup started in 1851, with the US winning for the first 132 years, before which country took the cup in 1983?

6. On 13 November 2008, the Michigan State team broke which team's incredible 1,270 games winning streak?

7. Which female high jumper competed between 1956 and 1967, never losing a competition, won two Olympic golds and improved her world record 14 times?

8. Which boxer with 50 consecutive winning bouts announced his retirement in 2017 after defeating Conor McGregor?

9. Which Australian racehorse finished her career in 2019, after winning 33 consecutive races?

10. Which team ended Liverpool's 44 game unbeaten Premier League run at the end of February 2020?

43. I CAN NEVER DO CRYPTIC CROSSWORDS

1. A post war Derby winner who was obviously not a wooden horse....?

2. A competitor in sport but especially here in golf....?

3. Did this commentator really carry his "Balls" all the way from Newcastle?

4. A father and son, both England Test cricketers, who would surely been more at home in the network of navigable rivers in Norfolk and Suffolk....?

5. It sounds as if this world speedway champion has been promoted from captain....?

6. A former England centre three-quarter: beech, ash, apple, lime, oak, elm, rowan, sycamore, fir, willow, birch, pear....?

7. This darts player's nickname suggests he is just as partial to lager as he is to cider....?

8. A former Welsh goalkeeper whose starting price comes before the commission taken by a casino when starting a poker game....?

9. A cricket umpire whose record 38 years on the first-class list confirmed that his decision never wavered....?

10. To bring up a university lecturer results in a six times world snooker champion....?

44. CACKHANDERS

1. Who was known as "Little Mo", and won nine Grand Slam singles titles in the early 1950's, becoming in 1953 the first woman to win all four Grand Slam tournaments in the same calendar year? However, in the following year a serious horse-riding accident ended her career.

2. Which overseas left-handed batsman is the current president of MCC, the first non-British president since the club was founded in 1787?

3. What are the only two sports which you are not allowed to play left-handed?

4. Who started his career as a star left-handed pitcher for the Boston Red Sox, but achieved his greatest fame as a slugging outfielder for the New York Yankees, setting batting records galore and being regarded as one of the greatest heroes in American culture?

5. Which left-handed darts player, now known as The Machine, in 2006 became the first player to hit three tournament nine dart finishes in a calendar year?

6. Who in 1963 became the first left-handed golfer to win the Open Championship, after beating Phil Rodgers in a play off?

7. Which left-handed snooker player was a childhood friend of fellow left-hander Jimmy White, and at 17 became the then youngest player to make a maximum break of 147?

8. Which Chinese badminton player, widely regarded as the greatest player of all time, is a six time All England champion, twice Olympic Champion, and five times world champion?

9. Which left arm bowler has taken the most wickets in Test cricket (433)?

10. Which left-handed tennis player has won a record 12 French Opens, and a record 59 Titles on clay?

45. KEEP YOUR HEAD ABOVE WATER

1. Who owned the yacht Morning Cloud?

2. Who in 1875 became the first person to swim the English Channel, and in 1883 died trying to swim the Whirlpool Rapids below Niagara Falls?

3. Where in this country is the National Water Sports Centre?

4. At what sport did Great Britain win an Olympic team gold medal in 1900, 1908, 1912 and 1920?

5. Which former rower, who has five Olympic medals, was appointed as chair of UK Sport in 2017?

6. On what river in 1922 did Georgina Ballantine catch the largest salmon ever recorded in British waters?

7. Which football league ground is passed by the crews in the annual Oxford v Cambridge boat race?

8. In canoeing what was the canoe slalom previously known as, reflecting as it did the nature of the course?

9. On what lake in 1967 did Donald Campbell crash and die whilst attempting to break the world water speed record?

10. Which British swimmer is the current Olympic champion, eight time world champion, twelve times European champion, and three times Commonwealth champion?

HALF TIME ENTERTAINMENT

Not quite on the lavish scale of the Super Bowl, but a change of format for ten rounds.

46. Name the ten managers to have led their clubs to Premier League championships.

47. Name the last ten winners of the Open Golf Championship.

48. Name the ten Britons to have won the Formula 1 Grand Prix drivers' championship.

49. Name the last ten cities to host the Summer Olympics.

50. Name the top ten Test run scorers of all time.

51. Name the top ten jockeys in the 2019-20 National Hunt season.

52. Name the top ten all-time points scorers in the history of the National Basketball Association.

53. Name the top ten Premiership rugby try scorers of all time.

54. Name the last ten women to win BBC Sports Personality of the Year.

55. Rod Laver and John Newcombe won two each of the first four Wimbledon Men's Singles championships of the Open era. Name the ten men to have won Wimbledon more than once since then.

Now you're ready for the second half!

56. NO MAN IS AN ISLAND

1. Mark Cavendish has won 30 Tour de France stages, putting him second on the all-time list, but which island has he represented in the Commonwealth Games?

2. What is the name of the only racecourse on Hong King island?

3. Dwayne Leverock came to prominence for a stunning catch at the 2007 cricket World Cup, more notable as he was the largest player in the tournament, weighing in at 20 stones. Which country was he representing?

4. Who caused a shock in 2002 when they held Scotland to a 2-2 draw in the qualifying competition for the Euro 2004 championships?

5. The Island Games are an international multi-sports event organised for competitor teams representing different island communities. 24 islands took part in the 2019 games, where were they held?

6. John Arlott, the renowned cricket broadcaster and writer, is buried in which small island's cemetery, where his headstone bears his very own words, "So clear you see those timeless things, like a bird the vision sings"?

7. Graeme Le Saux won 36 England caps, and played over 250 games for Chelsea, but where was he born?

8. Fe'ao Vunipola, father of Mako and Billy, represented which country in the 1995 and 1999 rugby World Cups?

9. Where did the 4-day cricket county championship game between Hampshire and Nottinghamshire in 2019 take place?

10. Which island in the outer Firth of Clyde, which is also a bird sanctuary, provides the granite for 60-70% of the world's curling stones?

57. LAND OF MY FATHERS

1. Which Welshman, the brother of actress Suzanne Packer (who played Tess Bateman in Casualty), had the reggae band Aswad name check him in their 1994 song "Shine" – his name is missing from the brackets?
   "Him a floating like a butterfly, the hurdling man
   Yes, me a chat about [   ]"?

2. Which jockey rode Earth Summit to win the unique treble of the Scottish, Welsh and English Grand Nationals?

3. Which British event rider, born in Chepstow in 1938, was a triple Olympic gold medallist and the first British rider to win an individual Olympic title?

4. Which world champion boxer retired in 2003 after an undefeated 46 contests, becoming one of only 15 world champions to retire undefeated?

5. Who was made a life-peer in 2010, swearing the oath of allegiance in both English and in Welsh, having previously in her career won 11 Paralympic gold medals and six London Marathons?

6. Who at Cardiff Arms Park in a match against Scotland in 1986 kicked the longest ever recorded penalty goal in an international rugby match, a kick measuring 70 yards 8½ inches?

7. Who played rugby for Cambridge University, Neath and Gloucester, prior to going on to captain England at cricket, and was the last man to captain England on his Test debut?

8. Who made his full debut for Wales at the age of 16, and in 2013 was transferred abroad for what was then a world record fee, with his new club eclipsing the amount they had previously paid for Cristiano Ronaldo?

9. What in 2009 became the first new National Hunt course to be built in UK for 80 years?

10. Who captained Great Britain's Ryder Cup team in 1957, the only time the US team suffered a defeat between 1933 and 1985, and was also named BBC Sports Personality of the Year for 1957?

58. WHERE WOULD YOU BE

1. On which golf course might you have to extricate yourself from the Hell Bunker?

2. Which football team would you support if, ironically, you watched your home games at Rugby Park?

3. At which sporting event do the competitors cross the Luckington Lane?

4. Which club rugby ground, demolished in 2010, would you associate with the singing of the folk song "Sosban Fach"?

5. If you were spectating at Maggotts, at which sporting venue would you be?

6. On what racecourse would you be riding if you climbed 73 feet from the lowest point, Swinley Bottom, to the winning post?

7. Where in London, since 1864, might you compete annually on Christmas Day over a 100 yard course for the Peter Pan Cup?

8. Where would you be watching a Formula 1 Grand Prix if you saw the cars negotiate the Swimming Pool chicane?

9. Which sport do you associate with the Waterloo Cup which was competed for annually on the Altcar Estate until 2005, at which date the sport became illegal?

10. If you were running in from the Kirkstall Lane End, at which sporting venue would you be playing?

59. MORE GENUINE ALL-ROUNDERS

1. Which British woman was a silver medallist in the quadruple sculls at the 2004 Olympics, won a gold in the same event at the 2005 world rowing championships, and then turned to cycling, winning a gold medal in the individual pursuit at the 2008 Olympics?

2. Who played 12 Tests for New Zealand at rugby league between 2004 and 2013, played 58 times for the All Blacks, and was also the New Zealand heavyweight boxing champion in 2012?

3. Which woman won gold medals at 80m hurdles and the javelin at the 1932 Olympics, excelled at basketball and baseball, and then went on to win ten tournaments on the LPGA tour?

4. Who was an Irish war-time champion at 100 yards and the long jump, and in 1946 on successive weekends played rugby for Ireland against France and soccer for an Ireland XI against Scotland?

5. Who first won an Olympic silver medal at ice hockey for Czechoslovakia, and then won the Wimbledon Men's Singles title in 1954 under his Egyptian citizenship?

6. Who was the AAA 100 yards champion in 1956, and then won nine England rugby caps on the wing between 1956 and 1961?

7. Who in 1975 finished the day 51 not out for Leicestershire against Derbyshire, headed to Doncaster Rovers to play in a 1-1 draw against Brentford, and returned next morning to complete a century and take three wickets as Leicestershire won their first County Championship title?

8. Which Formula 1 driver took up CART racing but, after losing both his legs in a horrific accident, designed and built his own custom legs, enabling him to win world series touring car races before winning gold medals at the 2012 and 2016 Paralympics?

9. Who, reputedly, turned down the throne of Albania, and on the sports field represented England at both cricket and football, and equalled the world record for the long jump?

10. Which ex-policeman is Great Britain's most capped international male athlete of all time (67 caps) excelling in the shot put, went on to twice win the title of "World's Strongest Man", won six Highland Games world championships, before becoming another world champion, in breeding budgerigars?

60. TURN OF THE CENTURY

1. Which athlete lit the flame in the Olympic cauldron at the 2000 Sydney games?

2. Which Sunderland player was the Premier League's top scorer in the 1999-2000 season with 30 goals?

3. Who made his Test debut in 2000 and went on to play 76 Tests in the next 6 years before a stress-related illness forced him to pull out of the national squad?

4. Who won the 2000 Grand National at his first attempt at the age of 20, riding Papillon, a horse trained by his father?

5. Who won the Ladies' Singles at Wimbledon in 2000, the first of her seven Grand Slam singles titles?

6. On which course did Tiger Woods win the 2000 US Open by 15 strokes, a record margin in any of the Majors?

7. Who do current records show as the winner of the general classification, ie the yellow jersey, in the 2000 Tour de France?

8. Italy joined rugby's Five Nations competition to make it Six Nations. Which Argentinian-born player scored 29 points as they beat Scotland in their first game in the competition?

9. Which Briton won the first of his four Olympic gold medals in the Sydney Olympic sailing competition?

10. To whom did England lose 1-0 in the last ever game at the old Wembley stadium in October, before it closed for rebuilding?

61. INITIALS FOR SPORTING PHRASES

Example: 1966 E WC W   1966 England World Cup Winners

1. 147 MB in S
2. 7 P for a T WC
3. 9 D F
4. 1954 F S F M M
5. 3 U P is an A
6. 400 H T S
7. 1780 F R of D
8. 5.5 W of S in G
9. 1 P for B in ARF
10. 4358 W R by TM

62. THE SILVER SCREEN – THE SEQUEL

1. Who won the 2009 Best Actress Oscar for her role in "The Blind Side", a biographical sports drama about the adoption of an impoverished young American footballer, and his college years leading to a pro career with the Baltimore Ravens?

2. The 1969 film "Downhill Racer" starred which Hollywood heartthrob as a skier who qualifies for the US Olympic team?

3. Which member of the cast of Gavin and Stacey starred in the 2018 British film "Swimming with Men", about an unlikely male synchronised swimming team who train for the world championships in Milan?

4. "Raging Bull" is a biopic of which middleweight boxer, with an Oscar-winning performance by Robert De Niro?

5. In the film "Invictus", about the 1995 rugby World Cup in South Africa, former Bath Rugby back-row forward Zak Fe'aunati played the part of which player?

6. 'One day in September' is a documentary film chronicling the events at which Summer Olympics?

7. Which iconic British-born American actor and comedian had a brief Boxing career (in 1919) under the name Packy East?

8. "Champions" is based on the story of which horse, the winner of the 1981 Grand National, who came back from chronic leg injuries, and its jockey Bob Champion, a testicular cancer survivor?

9. In the 2004 romcom "Wimbledon" starring Kirsten Dunst, John McEnroe and which other former champion appear, playing themselves as commentators?

10. What is the name of the 2019 documentary film covering the England Test cricket team between 2009 and 2013, as they rose from the depths of the rankings to become the world number one?

63. INJURY TIME

1. At which ground did Glenn McGrath step on a stray ball left on the outfield during the warm-up for an Ashes Test in 2005, damaging ankle ligaments, and possibly changing the course of the series?

2. Which Chelsea goalkeeper (previously with Wimbledon) dropped a jar of salad cream, instinctively stuck out a foot to save it and severed a tendon in his big toe?

3. Which bone did David Beckham break in 2002, causing a nation to hold its breath about his ability to play in that summer's World Cup finals?

4. Which 1993 Ryder Cup player tripped over a plant pot whilst sleepwalking during the competition, and sustained a toe and chest injury that ruled him out of the singles?

5. Following her win at Wimbledon in 2010, which tennis player was in a bar in Munich when she gashed her foot on a beer bottle (which had reportedly been dropped in a crowd watching a World Cup football match), and was out of the game for several months?

6. Which former Essex and England cricketer, now a respected writer, had to pull out of a 1980s Test match when he put his back out typing a letter?

7. Another unfortunate goalkeeper, who in 1975 shouted so violently at his Manchester United defence that he dislocated his own jaw?

8. In 2019 how did Welsh international and Ospreys rugby player, Scott Baldwin, get injured during a team trip to Weltevrede game lodge near Bloemfontein?

9. Which English spin bowler lost four toes while swimming in an accident involving a boat propeller, when on tour in the West Indies in 1968?

10. Final goalkeeping injury, but not amusing this time: which Manchester City goalkeeper broke his neck in the 1956 FA Cup Final?

64. AUF WIEDERSEHEN PET

1. Who was the most successful male backstroke swimmer of all time, winning four European and three world championships in a row, and setting 19 world records?

2. Which sometime controversial tennis player won six grand slams and, after his retirement, participated in professional poker tournaments prior to being declared bankrupt, a status extended to 2031?

3. Who captained the German football team when they lost the 1966 World Cup final to England, and was the first player to score a goal at four successive World Cup finals?

4. Who lost in three consecutive Wimbledon singles finals from 1935 to 1937, was imprisoned on morals charges, and then saw action on the Eastern Front and was awarded the Iron Cross?

5. Which showjumper won five Olympic gold medals, and actually won medals at six different Olympic Games?

6. Which golfer sank a putt on the 18th hole to assure his team's victory at "The Miracle of Medinah"?

7. Who became the first boxer ever to win the world heavyweight championship on a foul, when Jack Sharkey was disqualified?

8. Who is the only woman to have won two Olympic gold medals in the long jump, at the Olympics in 1992 and 2000, having previously won Olympic sprinting medals in 1988?

9. Which high profile football manager played 325 games for Mainz, before retiring in 2001 and immediately taking over as manager?

10. Which player, born in Poland, is his country's highest ever goal scorer, breaking Gerd Muller's record?

65. AROUND THE HOUSE

1. What was the nickname of William Perry who played for ten years as a defensive lineman in the NFL, weighed just under 24 stones, and also appeared at Wrestlemania?

2. Which father and son have played county cricket for Gloucestershire in the last sixty years?

3. Which prop has played nearly 100 games for the Wallabies, scoring just one try?

4. Who is the only sprinter to win the Olympic 100 metres and 200 metres at three consecutive Olympic games?

5. What is the name of the tallest fence on the Grand National course?

6. What is the first name of the Swedish tennis player who is one of only six men to have won Grand Slam singles titles on grass, hard and clay courts?

7. Which Premiership rugby club play at the Recreation Ground?

8. Who played county cricket for Somerset, before becoming a Test match umpire?

9. What indoor game relies heavily on the art of quality drawing woods?

10. Which winner of the Men's Singles title at Wimbledon in 1987, started the tradition of climbing into the stands to celebrate with his family and supporters?

66. THE COMMENTATOR'S CURSE

1. When Jonathan Agnew suggested that Ian Botham had been dismissed hit wicket because he had 'failed to get his leg over', he triggered one of the longest fits of barely suppressed giggles on the radio from which fellow commentator?

2. Which lyrical commentator said with reference to a darts player: "When Alexander of Macedonia was 33, he cried salt tears because there were no more worlds left to conquer. Bristow is only 27!"

3. "Kirkpatrick to Williams... This is great stuff. Phil Bennett covering, chased by Alistair Scown... Brilliant, Oh, that's brilliant. John Williams. Pullin, xxxx. Great dummy. David, Tom David, the half-way line. Brilliant by Quinnell. This is Gareth Edwards. A dramatic start. What a score!" Which player's name has been replaced by xxxx in Cliff Morgan's commentary of 'that try' from the 1973 game between the Barbarians and the All Blacks?

4. Which tennis commentator's favourite phrase – and he covered Wimbledon for 43 consecutive years – was "Oh I say!?"?

5. Commentators are supposed to remain impartial, but when England's hockey team at the 1988 Seoul Olympics went into a 3-1 lead to clinch the gold medal, which commentator declared "And where were the Germans? ...but frankly who cares!"?

6. The same commentator, back on familiar territory covering football, had another piece of over the top enthusiasm with this gem: "Interesting... VERY interesting! Look at his face! Just look at his face!" Who had just scored for Derby against his old club Manchester City?

7. There are a few variants on this quote, in the days before everyone had colour TVs: "The yellow is on the side cushion, and for those of you watching in black and white, it's just behind the blue" but who was the commentator?

8. "Lord Nelson! Lord Beaverbrook! Sir Winston Churchill! Sir Anthony Eden! Clement Attlee! Henry Cooper! Lady Diana! Maggie Thatcher - can you hear me, Maggie Thatcher! Your boys took one hell of a beating!" Who had just beaten England 2-1 in a 1981 World Cup qualifier to leave one local commentator slightly excited?

9. Which Cuban athlete at the 1976 Olympic Games "opened up his legs and showed his class" according to David Coleman?

10. "It is only 12 inches high... It is solid gold... And it undeniably means England are the champions of the world" Commentator and year?

67. THE SPORTING DICTIONARY

1. At what sport would you perform "a Rudolph and a Randolph"?

2. At what sport might you "throw stones at houses"?

3. At what sport might you start at the "south stake"?

4. In which two sports might you be penalised for "travelling"?

5. At what sport might you "trim your sheets"?

6. In which sport might you deliver "strokers", "crackers" or "tweeners"?

7. Which game starts with a "face off"?

8. At what sport might you use an "over and under" or a "side by side" in competition?

9. At what sport would the "golden score" rule be introduced if your score was equal to that of your opponent at the end of the match?

10. At what sport do you "weigh out" and later "weigh in"?

68. AND IN THE BEGINNING

1. Whose autobiography was entitled "I Had A Hammer", and is a play on his nickname "Hammering Hank", a legendary baseball player, who hit at least 24 home runs every year between 1954 and 1976?

2. Who is the only British heavyweight boxer to win both a gold medal at the Olympics, and then a world title sanctioned by a major professional body?

3. Who in two successive Test matches against Australia ran out Ian Meckiff with a direct hit to create the first ever tied Test, and then was out "hit wicket" after his cap fell on the stumps?

4. Which current Reading player, and a Scottish international, began his career with Rangers before being "loaned out" to Blackpool, where he was sent off on his debut?

5. Who first made his name in television playing private investigator Eddie Shoestring, is a keen Chelsea supporter, and in 1995 was seriously injured when he fell badly from his pony whilst playing polo?

6. Which fast bowler who played for Middlesex between 1977 and 1988, was nicknamed "Diamond", and once took 7-12, then an English domestic one day bowling record?

7. What was the name of the burger which McDonald's New Zealand created in 1996 when a certain rugby player, perhaps the first true global rugby superstar, was diagnosed with a rare and serious kidney disorder?

8. Who on 28 November 2018 scored four goals for Aston Villa when they drew 5-5 with Nottingham Forest?

9. Which tennis player, winner of the French Open in 1983 and the son of a Cameroon footballer, then became a popular singer, once performing a concert at the Stade de France attended by 80,000 people?

10. Which athlete won 122 consecutive races between 1977 and 1987 and set the world record in his event on four occasions?

69. ANCIENT AND MODERN

1. Who at the age of 14 won five gold medals at the 1976 Montreal Olympics, and became the first gymnast to achieve a perfect 10 in Olympic competition?

2. Who in 1997 became the youngest tennis player to win a Grand Slam title, at the age of 16 years and 117 days?

3. Who played in his first world snooker championship in 1937, and in his last 52 years later at the age of 75?

4. How old was Pele when, in Sweden in 1958, he became the youngest player to score a World Cup hat trick, and the youngest player to score in a World Cup final?

5. How old was Wilfred Rhodes when, in his final Test in 1930, he became the oldest player who has appeared in a Test match?

6. Who in 1976 beat WBA light welterweight champion Antonio Cervantes to become the youngest ever world boxing champion at the age of 17?

7. Swede Oscar Swahn holds records as the oldest Olympian at the time of competition, the oldest person to win gold, and the oldest person to win an Olympic medal. In which sport did he compete?

8. Who is the youngest player to compete in the Ryder Cup, being 19 years 8 months and 15 days old when he represented Europe in 1999?

9. Which goalkeeper, playing for Manchester City in 1995, became the oldest player to appear in the Premier League at the age of 43 years and 163 days?

10. Who is the oldest jockey to win the Grand National, partnering Grittar to victory in 1982 at the age of 48?

70. SCOTLAND THE BRAVE

1. Which jockey who rode 3,823 winners in his career, passing 100 winners in a season 17 times, joined Bill Beaumont as one of the captains on A Question of Sport, and also became chairman of Swindon Town?

2. Who is the only England cricket captain to be born in Scotland?

3. Who was Formula 1 world champion in 1963 and 1965, but was sadly killed after crashing in a Formula 2 race at Hockenheimring?

4. Eve Muirhead has competed in three Winter Olympics in which sport, winning a bronze medal with her team in Sochi in 2014?

5. Which golfer won the Open in 1985, and the Masters in 1988?

6. Who in 1995 became the first Scottish driver to win the World Rally Drivers' title, but died in 2007 when his helicopter crashed close to his family home near Lanark?

7. Which swimmer, who took pride in wearing his MacGregor tartan dressing gown poolside, is still the youngest winner of the BBC Sports Personality of the Year award, which he won at the age of 17?

8. What was the last Scottish trained horse to win the Grand National?

9. Jamie Gillan, nicknamed "the Scottish Hammer", made a major breakthrough in which sport in 2019?

10. The cabers that are tossed at the Highland Games are normally made from which wood?

61

71. SPORTING DISASTERS

1. Which world champion died at the 1994 San Marino Grand Prix, whilst he was leading the race, the crash coming the day after Roland Ratzenberger had crashed and died during qualification?

2. At which Olympic Games did the Palestinian terrorist group Black September kill eleven Israeli team members?

3. At which stadium were 39 Juventus fans killed prior to kick-off of the 1985 European Cup Final between Juventus and Liverpool?

4. At which Hong Kong racecourse in 1918 did 614 spectators lose their lives after a fire broke out?

5. Which British cyclist collapsed and died during the 1967 Tour de France?

6. Eight players and three staff members of Manchester United were killed when their plane failed to take off from which airport in February 1958?

7. Who was the Chelsea vice-chairman, and investor of £43 million into the club, who died when his helicopter crashed flying back from a game at Bolton?

8. Where did Pierre Levegh crash in 1955, with 83 spectators also being killed, after parts of his car catapulted into the crowd?

9. Which jockey, whose brother's nickname was "Smokin' Joe", was thrown from his horse at Ascot and fatally kicked on the head?

10. Which Test cricketer was hit on the neck by a bouncer during a Sheffield Shield match in 2014, and died in hospital a few days later?

72. KEEP IT IN THE FAMILY

1. Which sisters have won 14 Grand Slam tennis doubles titles and three Olympic gold medals as a pair?

2. Which rugby full back who played 19 times for England between 1961 and 1964 had a sister who won the Badminton three-day event on three successive occasions between 1957 and 1959?

3. Which two sisters were part of the British Gymnastics Team at the 2016 Olympics?

4. Which British twins played in five consecutive ladies doubles world championship table tennis finals between 1951 and 1955, twice winning gold and three times silver?

5. Which current trainer has three sons who are professional jockeys, one a champion flat jockey, and two steeplechase jockeys, and a daughter who is a racing television presenter?

6. Which Scottish commentator and broadcaster had two daughters, one of whom married former Scotland scrum half Alan Lawson and the other married horse racing commentator Derek Thompson?

7. Which mother and daughter, both international cyclists who both represented Great Britain at the 1972 world championships, set a British ten-mile record for women riding a tandem bicycle?

8. Who played in England women's football team at the 2019 World Cup, and has a sister Natasha who was the first ever British female boxer to compete at the Olympic Games?

9. Which female jockey finished third on Seabass in the 2012 Grand National, the best ever placing by a female jockey, and has a brother who rode 59 Cheltenham Festival winners?

10. Which former British number one ladies tennis player has a brother who represented Scotland at U21 football and a father who played football for the Soviet Union?

73. DID IT REALLY HAPPEN?

1. Who failed to score a point in his first world speedway final in 1971, yet won the final at his second attempt in 1973?

2. Which British tennis pair took 6 hours and 23 minutes to beat Charlie Pasarell and Ron Holmberg 26-24, 17-19, 30-28 in Maryland in 1968?

3. Pierre Etchebaster retired at the age of 60, after being undefeated world champion from 1928 to 1954 in which sport?

4. Exactly where did Alan Shepard hit a very special golf shot on 6 February 1971?

5. Between 1950 and 1953 which player made 62 football league appearances for Sheffield Wednesday, scoring 61 goals, before a tragic collision with Preston goalkeeper George Thompson resulted in a very serious leg injury which ended his career?

6. Which Somerset cricketer's benefit match at Bath in 1953 proved a financial disaster, despite the beneficiary taking 6-41, as it was over by 6pm on the first day?

7. Which second row forward scored his first International try in his 62nd game against France in 1975?

8. Which two Epsom Derby favourites, in 1960 and 1962, both fell at Tattenham Corner?

9. Who in 1950 as the British bantamweight champion, was knocked down 10 times in a European title fight, and then 14 times in a world title fight later in the same year?

10. Which British athlete entered the stadium in the marathon at the 1954 Vancouver Commonwealth Games 17 minutes in front of his nearest pursuer, yet took 11 minutes to stagger the next 200 yards before collapsing on the track, and was to never race again?

74. DOWN ON THE FARM

1. The League Cup changed its name to what in 1982, when it became the first major cup to be sponsored in English football?

2. Junior cricket bat sizes range from 0-6, but what name is given to the size of bat which ideally suits juniors of heights 163-168cms (5'4"-5'6")?

3. What is the better known name of the wrestler christened Martin Austin Ruane, who was British heavyweight champion weighing in from 31 stones at the beginning of his career to 49 stones 13lbs at the end?

4. In 2014 which Northern Ireland pole vaulter was awarded the accolade of being "Britain's greatest ever pole vaulter"?

5. Which football team used to play at the "Old" Plough Lane, and will return to the "New" Plough Lane next season?

6. ………… and what "Derby" used to be run over the ground that is being developed for the new Plough Lane?

7. Notts County played football until 1910 at Trent Bridge as tenants of Nottinghamshire county cricket club until they moved to which ground?

8. Nairn Suleymanoglu, nicknamed "The Pocket Hercules", is widely considered as the best pound for pound weightlifter of all time; and is the only weightlifter to date to clean and jerk 10kgs more than triple his bodyweight. He was born in Bulgaria, but on a trip to the World Cup final in Melbourne in 1986, he escaped his handlers and defected to which country?

9. Nayel Nassar, one of the world's leading show jumpers, living in the US but competing for Egypt, has recently become engaged to the daughter of which American business magnate?

10. If you were a batsman of somewhat limited technique, to what area of the field might your somewhat "agricultural" shots be heading?

75. CENTRAL EUROPE

1. Which Austrian with twenty-six downhill skiing wins is arguably the greatest downhill racer ever, having been inspired by the serious skiing injury suffered by his younger brother, Klaus, who was paralysed from the waist down?

2. Which nation missed five Olympics but has still won the Olympic water polo title a record nine times? As of today, there are only seven major water polo tournaments in which they have participated but did not receive a medal?

3. In a Peanuts cartoon in 1973 Snoopy is seen doing flawless gymnastics on top of his doghouse saying at the end, "— — has been begging me for lessons". Who was the "Sparrow from Minsk" he was referring to, who had redefined gymnastics at the 1972 Olympics?

4. Where in Switzerland would you watch the White Turf horse racing meeting over three weekends in February each year?

5. Which Polish rider was the 2019 world individual speedway champion?

6. Which Czech athlete is regarded as the greatest javelin thrower of all time, having made 52 of the total 84 throws that have cracked the elusive 90m barrier?

7. Who, according to Billie Jean King is "the greatest singles, doubles, mixed doubles player ever" with an astounding 59 grand slams, having asked for political asylum in New York very early in her career before embarking on the most career victories that tennis has ever seen?

8. Who was born in Budapest in 1911, moved to America before joining the British army as a parachutist to fight against the Nazis in Yugoslavia, and then proceeded to win twenty English open table tennis tittles and five world championship titles?

9. Hungary beat England 6-3 at Wembley in 1953 and then did so again 7-1 in the return fixture in 1954. Who was the English goalkeeper who conceded all 13 goals?

10. Which Czech runner is the only Olympic athlete whose statue appears at the Olympic Museum in Lausanne? At the 1952 Olympics he completed the unique treble of winning the 5,000m, the 10,000m and the Marathon.

76. CAN'T SEE THE WOOD FOR THE TREES

1. What is the name of the Classic Group 1 flat race, run at Epsom, which is only open to three-year old fillies?

2. Who played 679 games for Huddersfield Town, Leeds United and Bradford City between 1965 and 1985, 27 times for England, and was the first England player to receive a red card in a friendly International? He died in April 2020.

3. What is the name given to the 18th hole at Augusta, Georgia?

4. What is the nickname of the legendary All Black lock Colin Meads?

5. Who in 1958 became the UK's first Formula 1 world champion, yet within three months of his retirement was killed in a car crash on the Guildford bypass?

6. What is the name of Motherwell FC's home ground?

7. On what overseas Test cricket ground might you watch the game from under the scoreboard, sitting on the Oaks Grass Embankment?

8. What is the name of the Toronto ice hockey club that has won the Stanley Cup 13 times, the second highest number of all teams? Yet their last win was in 1967, giving them the longest current drought in the NHL.

9. Which leading international sportsman has the Christian names Eldrick Tont?

10. When David Hemery won his gold medal at the 1968 Olympics which British athlete won the bronze, causing David Coleman to utter one of his famous Colemanballs:
    "Who cares who's third – it doesn't matter"?

77. PIPPED AT THE POST

1. Over 2,000 Test cricket matches have been played, but only two have ever been tied. Australia featured in both, but who were their opponents in the second one?

2. When Manchester United came from behind to beat Bayern Munich 2-1 to win the 1999 Champions League final, two substitutes each scored in injury time to capture the treble for United. Who were those two goalscorers?

3. The 2012 Ryder Cup has been called the Miracle at Medinah. Europe were 10-4 down with two fourballs to complete and the singles to be played, but eventually won 14½-13½. Who added to the drama on the final day by oversleeping and needing a police escort to make his singles tee time?

4. In 2008 Lewis Hamilton needed to finish at least fifth in the final race in Brazil to win the F1 title, but was having a poor race and struggling to achieve this place. His main rival crossed the finish line first and, at that point, would have been world champion, only for Hamilton to move up from sixth to fifth on the penultimate corner to snatch the title. Who was that rival, competing in his home Grand Prix?

5. Which horse held off Santini's strong finish to win the 2020 Cheltenham Gold Cup, retaining the title won in 2019?

6. In the 2003 rugby World Cup final, Jonny Wilkinson dropped the goal in the last minute of extra-time to put England into the lead. After the restart, which England player put the ball into touch with the last kick of the match?

7. Name either of the British sprinters who tied for first place and the gold medal at the 1982 Commonwealth Games 200m, a rarity with today's high-speed photo finish cameras?

8. Who led the 2017 Super Bowl 28-9 at the end of the third quarter, only for the New England Patriots to stage a remarkable comeback to win 34-28 in overtime?

9. Who missed a conversion in front of the posts with the last kick of the game in the 1968 rugby league cup final at a waterlogged Wembley, which would have given Wakefield Trinity victory? He missed, Leeds won 11-10, and Eddie Waring memorably described the kicker as 'the poor lad.'

10. At last year's cricket World Cup final New Zealand needed two to win from the last ball of the super over. Which England player fielded the ball on the boundary and threw to Jos Buttler for the wicketkeeper to complete the run out which meant that England won?

78. THE WHEEL OF FORTUNE

1. Which cyclist, who retired in 2013, jointly holds the British record for the most Olympic gold medals with six?

2. Where might you speed down the Mulsanne Straight?

3. Since 1975, the Tour de France leader travels up which famous street to cross the finishing line?

4. Around which racecourse was the British Grand Prix run five times between 1955 and 1962?

5. Richard Petty is known as the King of Nascar, but what is his sport?

6. Which British rider was speedway world individual champion in 2013, 2015 and 2018?

7. Which British wheelchair athlete won a total of six gold medals at the 2008 and 2012 Paralympic Games, and has won the London marathon on eight occasions?

8. Which driver currently holds the record for the most Grand Prix victories, having won 91 races?

9. Which race, held in late May each year, on a track nicknamed "The Brickyard" is said to attract nearly 300,000 spectators?

10. Who is the only person to have won world championships on both two and four wheels?

79. TOP OF THE CLASS

1. The Old Carthusians won the FA Cup in 1881 – they were the old boys of which school?

2. What English public school has played host to an annual cricket festival since 1872, making it the longest running cricket festival in the world?

3. England Test cricket captain, Peter May, won the Kinnaird Cup on three occasions with his brother. What sport were they playing?

4. William Webb Ellis famously picked up a ball and ran with it at which school in 1823?

5. Which school includes, among its many sporting scholars, Mary Rand, Chris Robshaw, Duncan Goodhew, Tyrone Mings and Lando Norris?

6. At which school did thirteen-years old AEJ Collins make the highest ever recorded individual cricket score of 628 not out?

7. Which two current international rugby colleagues both went to St George's School in Harpenden?

8. The game of quidditch, a wizarding sport played on broomsticks, is associated with which school?

9. Which public school was attended by leading flat racehorse trainers, William Haggas and Sir Mark Prescott; and by current rugby Internationals, Maro Itoje and Mako Vunipola?

10. Which school provided three members of England's recent international cricket teams?

80 THE SPANISH INQUISITION

1. Which motor cycle racer finished the 2019 season with a record points tally of 420, the most ever by any rider in a single season and is one of only four riders (along with Mike Hailwood, Phil Read and Valentino Rossi) to have won world championship titles in three different categories?

2. Who won five successive Tours de France between 1991 and 1995, the only rider to achieve that numbers of victories consecutively?

3. Which female tennis player won six Grand Slam doubles titles, including Wimbledon in 1995 with Jana Novotna, and is also the only tennis player to play in five Olympic games?

4. Who is generally regarded as the greatest European golfer of all time, so much so that the European team's logo at the 2012 Ryder Cup was a silhouette of his famous salute following his 1984 Open win?

5. Which current Premier League manager holds the record for the most consecutive games won in La Liga, the Bundesliga and the Premier League?

6. Who was the Spanish squash champion at the age of 16, had a trial as a footballer with Real Madrid, but made his name as a rally driver winning the world title twice? (His son currently drives for McLaren in Formula 1)

7. Who became the highest paid matador in history, yet in 1964 on his first appearance in Madrid was nearly gored to death by the bull Impulsivo?

8. Who won the Le Mans 24 hours race in 2018 and 2019 having won the Formula 1 world championship in 2005 and 2006?

9. Which wrestler, born in Spain and christened Glenn Thomas Jacobs, is a three times world wrestling champion, the younger half-brother of the Undertaker, and is now the mayor of Knox County, Tennessee?

10. Who currently plays for the Japanese club Vissel Kobe, having played for 22 years at Barcelona, and been named in the FIFA FIFPro World XI nine times?

81. WAY BACK IN TIME

1. Of the five English horse racing classics, which was the latest to begin, its inaugural run being in 1814?

2. Where was the first and only Olympic games of the nineteenth century held?

3. Which sport was effectively born on 29 August 1895, when representatives of 22 clubs met in the George Hotel, Huddersfield?

4. Spencer Gore won what competition in its first playing in 1877?

5. Who is one of only five players to have represented both England and Australia in Test matches, and in 1884 scored the first ever Test double century?

6. The first university boat race between Oxford and Cambridge took place in 1829 as a result of a challenge between two former school friends. Where did it take place?

7. Which is the oldest 'open' rugby club in the world (by open meaning open to anyone, not merely those attending, or old boys from, a particular school, university or hospital) – founded in 1858, and open from 1862?

8. The twelve teams which were the founder members of the Football League in 1888 were predominantly northern, but which is situated the furthest east?

9. Boxing matches in the early days were originally conducted under the London Prize Ring rules, but in 1867 a new code of rules was established that still exists today. What is the name of these 'Rules'?

10. On which course were the first twelve Open golf championships played between 1860 and 1872, before course rotation began?

82. GONE FISHIN'

1. Which football club's nickname is the Addicks, the most likely origin being from a local fishmonger who rewarded the team with meals of haddock and chips?

2. Who has played cricket over 150 times for the West Indies across all formats, took a hat trick in the 2011 World Cup, and appeared for Worcestershire in the 2011 English season?

3. Who captained Scotland to victory in the famous 'winner takes all' Grand Slam rugby match against England in 1990?

4. Which golfer was known as the Great White Shark?

5. Four different body positions are allowed in diving; which involves bending the body at the waist and keeping the legs straight?

6. Which baseball player in 2019 signed what was reportedly the most lucrative deal in sport: a 12-year extension worth $426.5m (£324m) with the Los Angeles Angels?

7. Which species of fish is named after a famous 1920's heavyweight boxing champion, the name referring to its aggressive nature and strong facial features, likened to that of the boxer?

8. Following Rory Best's retirement, who started at hooker for Ireland in their first three 2020 Six Nations games?

9. Which jockey rode Imperial Aura to victory for trainer Kim Bailey at the 2020 Cheltenham Festival?

10. What nickname did Eric Moussambani, a swimmer from Equatorial Guinea, acquire at the 2000 Olympics in Sydney for completing his heat of 100m freestyle in the unprecedently slow time of 1:52.72, the slowest time in Olympic history by far?

83. FILM/TV – THE NAME'S THE SAME

From the film / TV programme on the left, one of the stars' surnames matches that of the sports star on the right.

1.	"The Dambusters"	A three-day event rider with multiple Olympic medals, spanning a remarkable 28 years
2.	"The Two Ronnies"	He was known as "Gentleman Jim", and in his final world heavyweight fight he was knocked out in round 23 by James J Jeffries
3.	"Little Women" (2019 version)	A left-handed American golfer, famed for his driving distances, and twice Masters winner – has also recently announced plans to run for Mayor of Pensacola
4.	"The Robe"	The first Englishman to be sent off in an international rugby match
5.	"Brideshead Revisited"	The presenter of "Sports Report" between 1955 and 1964, and also of "This Is Your Life" from 1955 to 1987
6.	"Dad's Army"	The first darts player to hit a televised nine dart finish
7.	"Saturday Night and Sunday Morning"	He played 76 times for England between 1946 and 1958 and his only league club was Preston North End
8.	"Harry Potter"	Three-time winner of both the London and New York marathons, and held the women's marathon world fastest time from 2003 to 2019
9.	"Car Share"	He was once Britain's most expensive footballer when transferred to Everton for £60,000 but in 1964 was banned from football for life and sent to prison for betting on a match
10.	"Killing Eve"	A massive 6' 8" England second row forward who played for Bristol, Wasps and Toulon

84. MARITAL BLISS

1. Ann Packer won the 800m gold and broke the world record at the 1964 Tokyo Olympics. Who did she marry that year – he was captain of the GB Olympic athletics team, and won a silver in the 4 x 400m relay?

2. Australian rugby union international Matt To'omua, who played for Leicester Tigers between 2016 and 2019, is married to which leading Australian cricketer who has also played soccer for her country?

3. Kate and Helen Richardson-Walsh won an Olympic gold medal together in which sport at the Rio Olympics in 2016?

4. Which former champion National Hunt jockey married trainer Henrietta Knight in 1995 having given her the ultimatum, "it's the bottle or me"?

5. One has a rugby World Cup winner's medal, the other has been BBC Sports Personality of the Year - which married couple?

6. Which former professional golfer was Chris Evert married to, for less than two years between 2008 and 2009?

7. Rugby presenter Sarra Elgan is the daughter of one former British Lion, Elgan Rees, and married to which other former Lion?

8. How many Olympic gold medals have Jason Kenny and Laura Trott won between them?

9. Alyssa Healy, an Australian international wicketkeeper like her uncle Ian, is married to which other Australian cricketer?

10. Anita Lonsbrough, who won a swimming gold at the 1960 Rome Olympics, is married to which former professional cyclist, who is now a respected commentator on his sport?

85. "AND I QUOTE"

Who said:

1. "In 1969 I gave up women and alcohol - it was the worst twenty minutes of my life."

2. "All Australians are an uneducated and unruly mob."

3. "After that, Des, even sex is an anti-climax!" (live on tv after riding the winner of the Grand National)

4. "The more I practise, the luckier I get."

5. "Pressure? I'll tell you what pressure is. Pressure is a Messerschmitt up your arse. Playing cricket is not. "

6. "Some people believe football is a matter of life and death. I'm very disappointed with that attitude. I can assure you it is much, much more important than that."

7. "I don't think we've met before, but I'm the referee on this field, not you. Stick to your job and I will do mine."

8. Which England cricketer was asked by an Australian fan "Can I borrow your brain? I'm building an idiot!"

9. "You can make a lot of money in this game. Just ask my ex-wives. Both of them are so rich that neither of their husbands work" (golfer)

10. "I wouldn't say I was the best manager in the business. But I was in the top one."

86. THE DRINKS CABINET

1. Who in 1977 was the first female jockey to ride in the Grand National?

2. Which brothers in the late 1890s became Gloucester's first England rugby union internationals?

3. Which Soviet fencer won gold at the 1980 Olympics in the foil event but was killed during a bout at the 1982 world championships when his opponent's sword broke on entering his mask?

4. Which is the only dog to win three successive greyhound Grand Nationals?

5. At what sport did Heather MacKay remain undefeated in competitive matches for 19 years between 1962 and 1981 and win 16 consecutive British Opens?

6. Who is the current manager of Feyenoord and has held 24 different managerial appointments including both countries and clubs? His last British club was Sunderland in 2015.

7. Who dropped five goals in a 1999 rugby World Cup quarter final match for South Africa to eliminate England?

8. Which Italian driver raced in 121 Formula 1 Grand Prix between 1984 and 1995, never winning a race, but did win Le Mans in 1999?

9. Which Hampshire batsman played 17 Tests for England between 1911 and 1928, and was the fourth-highest run scorer in all first-class cricket?

10. What trophy is presented annually to the winning golfer at the Open Championship?

87. STRANGE BUT TRUE

1. Which tourist in 1960 became the first bowler to take a hat-trick at Lord's but never played another Test match?

2. Who kept goal for Great Britain at the 1948 Olympics, yet did not win his first international cap for Scotland until the 1966-1967 football season?

3. Which Formula 1 driver did the stunt driving for the film "Grand Prix" at the Monte Carlo circuit, but ironically was killed in a crash in the Monaco Grand Prix at the same circuit the next year?

4. Who won the only world heavyweight boxing title fight to be staged on Boxing Day?

5. Which British Lion beat David Lloyd to win Junior Wimbledon in 1966?

6. Which cricketer, a well-known administrator, once made a century for England after 85 successive first-class innings of under 50?

7. Which Welsh international rugby player, who was capped between 1967 and 1974, a police officer by profession, scored a try against Pontypool in the morning, and another against Neath in the afternoon?

8. Frenchman Dr Ivan Osiier competed in the Olympic games over a record span of 40 years, between 1908 and 1948, but what was his sport?

9. Who rode Signal Box to be third in the 1951 Epsom Derby, just a few weeks after riding the winner of the Cheltenham Gold Cup?

10. Which Golfer won the Open Championship in 1953 by reducing his score by one stroke each round (72, 71, 70, 69) to score 282?

88. YOUR SATNAV MAY HELP

The postcode relating to each of the specific venues appears in the mixed-up list below. Pair up the appropriate postcode with its venue.

1. The venue due to stage the 2020 Open Golf championship

2. An historic rugby league ground that closed in 2019, having in 1954 hosted 102,569 spectators for a Challenge Cup final replay

3. The cricket ground where Gary Sobers once hit six sixes in an over

4. The venue for the annual world snooker championship

5. The National Horseracing Museum

6. A racecourse where notorious highwayman Dick Turpin was hanged in 1739

7. A premiership rugby ground in the only English city to also house a Premier League football club, a first-class county cricket ground and a racecourse

8. The Sir Chris Hoy velodrome also known as the Emirates Arena

9. An English football ground named St James' Park, housing over 50,000 spectators

10. An English football ground named St James Park, housing just over 8,000 spectators

A.	G40 3HG	F.	CT13 9PB
B.	EX4 6PX	G.	BD6 1BS
C.	S1 1DA	H.	YO23 1EX
D.	NE1 4ST	J.	SA2 0AR
E.	LE2 7TR	K.	CB8 8EP

89. THE NOBILITY

1. What was the name of the leading suffragette who was killed by King George V's horse, Anmer, at the 1913 Epsom Derby when she ducked under the rails and ran onto the course?

2. The RR are a franchise cricket team who won the very first IPL competition under captaincy of Shane Warne, but what does the RR stand for?

3. Which rider competed at six Olympic games between 1992 and 2012, and twice won the Badminton three-day event horse trials?

4. Who was the cox of the winning 1950 Cambridge boat race crew whose royal wedding was the first to be broadcast on television?

5. What professional football club plays its home games at Palmerston Park in Dumfries?

6. What racket sport derives its name from the seat of the Duke of Beaufort in Gloucestershire?

7. Which crime writer wrote over forty international best sellers yet his first book, his sporting autobiography, was entitled "The Sport of Queens"?

8. What sport's name is derived from the intentionally convex nature of the playing surface, which is traditionally formed with a raised centre?

9. Who are the only parent and child to have both won the Sports Personality of the Year award?

10. Which Russian Prince scored two tries on his England debut against the All Blacks in 1936 – the first try still being recalled as one of the greatest individual tries ever seen at Twickenham?

90. I WAS THERE (CHRIS'S OWN REMINISCENCES)

1. I was born in Solihull and as a young child my favourite uncle started taking me to watch Birmingham City. I was there when they recorded their 9-1 record score against which club?

2. As a Birmingham supporter I was disappointed not to attend the 1956 Cup Final v Manchester City, but I did go to Wembley the next year to watch Aston Villa v Manchester United. Which goalkeeper was carried off injured in this match?

3. After Wembley my next treat was Twickenham to watch England v Scotland and, after the harsh winter of 1963 and being snowed in at the Highwayman Inn near Birdlip for six weeks, I saw which England captain and fly-half score one of the most brilliant individual tries ever seen at Twickenham?

4. On a balmy summer evening in 1992 I was in Barcelona on a three day visit to the Olympics with Edward Gillespie. We sat on the very back row of the stand but luckily the men's 100m final took place down the straight in front of us. Who won that race?

5. I was at Exeter races in January 2005 to watch one of my own horses run. but in one of the other races a very promising young novice chaser priced at 2/1 in a three-horse race fell at the last when well clear. He was remounted and rapidly made up the deficit only to be pipped at the post by a short head. Who was that beaten horse who was later to win the Cheltenham Gold Cup?

6. Somewhere in this book there is reference to Jack Russell scoring his maiden first-class century in a test match against Australia. But when he scored his maiden century in club cricket for Stroud CC v Malmesbury CC who was the bowler who bowled the ball that Jack drove through mid-on for four to reach his hundred?

7. On Saturday 2nd September 1995 I was at Wembley stadium to see Frank Bruno win the world heavyweight championship, the first British boxer to do so on British soil. Who was his opponent?

8. Rather than just be there, I was actually at the wicket (at the non-striker's end) when Cheltenham CC needed six to win off the last ball to win the National Knockout Final at Lord's. David Locke defied the odds and hit the ball for six into what is the most famous public bar on the ground?

9. Another final at Lord's but this time Gloucestershire were playing in 2000 when I met up in the box with a former pupil, not a cricketer but still a Glos fan thanks to his days at Stouts Hill School. Who was this well-known actor/writer/TV presenter that I took up to the Glos dressing room to watch an hour's play with the team from the balcony?

10. I went along to the clay pigeon shooting finals at the Royal Artillery Barracks at the London Olympics to support brother Ian in his capacity as team manager of the British clay pigeon trap shooting team. Who was his shooter who won a gold medal?

91. THE MET OFFICE

1. Which rugby player, with a family background very much in the theatre, made 60 appearances for England between 2006 and 2014, and was christened Tobias Gerald Albert Cecil Lieven......?

2. Which cricket team, captained by Heather Knight, won the 2019 women's Super League?

3. What was the nickname of the boxer who lost to Joey Giardello in a world title fight in 1964, prior to being wrongfully convicted of murder, and was later released following a petition of habeas corpus after serving almost twenty years in prison?

4. Which horse won the 2015 Grand National, but sadly collapsed and died after winning the Cotswold Chase at Cheltenham in 2017?

5. Who in March 2019 became the first woman, the daughter of a former Grand National winning jockey, to win a Grade 1 race over obstacles at the Cheltenham Festival?

6. Which former England cricketer published two volumes of poetry after his retirement, with one poem being entitled "Lord's Test"?

7. Which defender made 636 Football League appearances between 1977 and 1998, appearing 300 times for West Ham, and 277 times for Fulham?

8. At what ground did umpire Dickie Bird abandon play for the day in June 1975 because of snow when Derbyshire were playing Lancashire?

9. What horse provided Vincent O'Brien with the first of his three successive Grand National winners from 1953 to 1955?

10. What is the nickname of the Finnish motor racing driver who won the Formula 1 world championship in 2007?

92. MRS BROWN'S BOYS

1. Which Scottish golfer played in five Ryder Cups between 1977 and 1987 and is now a respected broadcaster on his sport?

2. Which Jamaican woman won the Olympic 200m in both the 2004 and 2008 games, as well as six other Olympic medals?

3. Who was Tottenham Hotspur's goalkeeper during the 1960-61 double winning season, during which he only missed one game?

4. Which 11-year-old skateboarder, who performed at the 2019 Sports Personality of the Year awards, was set to become Britain's youngest ever Summer Olympics competitor at Tokyo 2020?

5. Which director of cricket led Warwickshire to wins in the 2014 T20 Blast and the Royal London one-day cup in 2016 before being sacked later that year?

6. Which wide receiver had nine successful seasons with the Pittsburgh Steelers but, following increasing disputes and allegations regarding off-field activities, made only one further appearance in 2019 despite high profile signings for two other teams?

7. Which Dutch woman swimmer won the 50m and 100m freestyle and the 100m butterfly at the Sydney Olympics, setting world records in all three events?

8. Which rugby player has over 70 England caps and has played over 300 times for his club, who in 2019 renamed one of the bars at their ground in his honour?

9. Which British archer won gold medals in the women's individual compound events at the 2008 and 2012 Paralympic games?

10. Who is regarded as the outstanding pioneering English rock climber of the 1950s and early 1960s, and made the first ascent of the world's third highest mountain, Kangchenjunga?

93. LONDON CALLING

1. London Irish rugby club are due to share a ground with which football club from the 2020-21 season?

2. Prior to the second world war there were some thirty greyhound tracks operating in and around London but which are the only two of these tracks remaining today?

3. Father Time is an iconic weathervane at Lord's Cricket Ground but what is he depicted as doing with his right hand on the vane?

4. Pall Mall, the well-known street in London, takes its name from the French game 'Paille-Maille', which translates into what in English?

5. London's oldest sports building still in use, and originally build for Cardinal Wolsey between 1526 and 1529, is a Real Tennis court where?

6. At which London stadium did Chris Chataway break the world 5000m record in 1954 and Derek Ibbotson break the world mile record in 1957?

7. In June 2019 the London Stadium hosted the first US Major League baseball game between which two teams?

8. Where is the London Broncos home ground?

9. Which venue hosted the first FA Cup Final and the first ever rugby union international to be played in England?

10. Chris Coley's debut for Cheltenham RFC in 1970 (he dropped a goal!) was against which current Premiership side at their ground, then in Repton Avenue, Sudbury, but they now play almost 100 miles away?

94. OUT OF AFRICA

1. Who was the first in a long line of successful middle and long distance runners to come from Kenya, winning the 1,500m gold medal at the 1968 Olympics in Mexico City?

2. Who was the captain of the 2019 Webb Ellis Cup winners?

3. Who is the only South African driver to win the South African Grand Prix?

4. Which Zimbabwean backstroke swimmer competed in five Olympic games between 2000 and 2016, winning seven Olympic medals, making her the most decorated Olympian from Africa?

5. Mo Salah currently plays for Liverpool but, when he first left his Egyptian native team, El Mokawloon, which European team did he join?

6. Who retired from athletics in May 2015, having finished only 16th in the Great Manchester Run, and so ended a 25 year career in which he claimed two Olympic gold medals, eight world championships, and set 27 world records?

7. With South African golfer, his brother a conservationist who saved the white rhino from extinction, became the only non- American to win all four Majors in a career?

8. Kevin Anderson lost to Novak Djokovic in the 2018 Wimbledon Men's final, but who had he beaten over five long sets (26-24 in the final set) in the semi-final, with the match lasting 6 hours and 36 minutes?

9. Who was the South African cricket captain who played in 19 Test Matches between 1951 and 1958, yet prior to this had played in the centre for England at rugby?

10. In what African city did Muhammad Ali knock out George Foreman to win the world heavyweight title in "The Rumble in The Jungle"?

95. I CAN SEE CLEARLY NOW

1. Which cricketer, a gutsy player of fast bowling, was voted BBC Sports Personality of the Year in 1975, the same year that he made his Test debut at Lord's at the age of 33 against the Australians?
He got lost in the pavilion when he went out to bat and found himself in the basement toilets.

2. Who won the world snooker championship in 1985, beating the favourite Steve Davis and coming back from 8-0 frames down to win the title on the final black of the 35th final frame with an estimated 18 million viewers watching television until after midnight?

3. Which Dutch footballer, capped 74 times and recognisable from his dreadlocked hair and the protective goggles he wore due to glaucoma, ended his career as player/manager of Barnet, and was booked in each of the first eight games he played?

4. Which American golfer won three US Opens, the last in 1990 when he became the oldest ever US champion at the age of 45, and has since been an outstanding player on the Seniors' tour, actually shooting a score less than his age in 2012?

5. Which cricketer, the only player to have scored more than 3,000 Test runs without a career century, has complete heterochromia, one blue and one green eye? He did once score 99 and his dismissal was later shown to have been from a delivery which should have been called as a no ball!

6. Which tennis player, aged 29 then, beat the 55-year-old Bobby Riggs in the "Battle of the Sexes" match at Houston Astrodome in 1973 in front of 30,000 spectators? (Both players wore glasses)

7. Which English bowler, generally regarded as one of the greatest bowlers of all times, won three world outdoor singles titles and three world indoor singles titles and in 1986 was crowned "Pipe Smoker of the Year"?

8. Which Irish born rugby player retired from the game after losing the sight in his left eye but, after finding he could wear specially designed goggles, returned to the game in Italy and in the last three years has won nine caps for the full national team?

9. Which cricketer in 2019 received free Specsavers glasses for life following his heroics supporting Ben Stokes in the dramatic Headingley Test?

10. Which bespectacled distance runner won European gold medals both before and after the second world war yet, despite being the obvious choice to carry the Olympic torch into the Wembley stadium for the 1948 Olympics, was turned away at the last moment as the organising committee wanted a more handsome athlete?

96. THE QUEEN'S CORONATION YEAR

1. Who scored a hat-trick in the "Matthews Cup Final" when Blackpool beat Bolton 4-3?

2. Randolph Turpin lost his world middleweight title to which American?

3. Which golfer won the Open Championship, the US Open and the Masters?

4. Jean Westwood and Lawrence Demmy of Great Britain were world champions in what sport?

5. Hillary and Tensing conquered Everest but who actually led the expedition, the news of its success reaching London on the morning of the coronation?

6. Which British rider was 500cc World Motor Cycling champion?

7. Which jockey, who was retiring at the end of the season and had recently been knighted, rode Pinza to win the Derby after 27 previous non-winning rides?

8. The horse that finished second to Pinza was named Aureole. Who was his owner?

9. England regained the Ashes at the Oval after a drought of twenty years under whose captaincy?

10. Which 18-year-old, never to win Wimbledon in his career, won the Australian and French open tennis championships?

97. WHEN THERE WAS STILL SPORT IN 2020

1. Which Manchester City and England midfielder with 149 England caps was awarded an MBE in the 2020 New Year Honours list?

2. Who went into 2020 as the number one ranked tennis player, meaning that he had achieved that feat in years across three different decades?

3. Who won the 2019-20 Conditional Jockeys championship forty years after his father last won the main jump jockeys title?

4. Who was the first England batsman to make a test century in 2020?

5. At the point at which the 2020 Six Nations paused, who was the competition's leading try scorer?

6. In which country was the first grand prix of the year scheduled to take place, and the first one to be cancelled?

7. As English football went into lockdown in March 2020, who was bottom of the English leagues, 24th in League Two?

8. Of the Five Cricketers of the Year announced in Wisden's 2020 Almanack, who was the only one not to play international cricket in 2019?

9. Who was the only British cyclist to win a gold medal at the 2020 Track Cycling World Championships in Berlin?

10. Which Welsh rugby international is part of the syndicate which owns Potters Corner, the winner of the 2020 Virtual Grand National trained by Christian Williams?

98. THE NHS

1. The United Hospitals Challenge Cup, contested by the six medical schools in London, is the oldest cup competition in the world in which sport?

2. What is the name of the welcome breeze which frequently provided relief from the afternoon heat at the WACA Test venue in Perth?

3. Which leading American ophthalmologist and professional tennis player was one of the first athletes to identify as transgender and was refused entry to Wimbledon in 1976?

4. Which doctor won an Olympic rowing gold medal prior to writing one of the best-selling books of all time "Baby and Child Care"?

5. Which West Indian batsman scored 258 against New Zealand in 1969, the highest score ever made by a cricketer in his final test innings?

6. Which Samoan rugby player, who was the first from any team to appear in five World Cups, gained the nickname "the Chiropractor" from his uncompromising tackling?

7. Which horse trained by Peter Chappell-Hyam won the 1992 Derby?

8. Who along with Jim Fox and Adrian Parker won the team gold medal in the modern pentathlon at the 1976 Olympics?

9. Dr Roger Bannister is famous for running the first sub four-minute mile but he only held the world record for 46 days before his time was beaten by which Australian athlete?

10. Which American speedway rider shares the same surname as the current Health Secretary, has won four world championships and retired in February 2020 having competed at the highest level in four decades?

99. THE LAST GOODBYES

1. Who made his final farewell to Golf, while standing on the iconic Swilcan Bridge at St Andrews, in the final round of the 2005 British Open?

2. Capard King, trained by Jonjo O'Neill, provided AP McCoy with the final winner of his professional racing career in April 2015, on which course?

3. Of the 15 players who started for England in the 2003 Rugby World Cup final, who was the last to retire from professional rugby?

4. Which broadcaster concluded his career so matter of factly at the Centenary Test in 1980 with the words: "9 runs off the over, 28 Boycott, 15 Gower, 69 for 2, and after Trevor Bailey it will be Christopher Martin-Jenkins"?

5. Which world champion heavyweight boxer decided early in his career to change his surname because ring announcers could never pronounce it correctly, but later retired with a perfect 49 fight record?

6. Best Mate won three successive Cheltenham Gold Cups between 2002 and 2004, but on which racecourse did he sadly collapse and die of a suspected heart attack in 2005?

7. Which cricketer on his final Test appearance in 2018 scored 147 and in doing so became only the fifth batsman to score a century in his first and last Test matches?

8. Which rugby player, the most capped by his country, was denied a final World Cup appearance by Typhoon Hagibis?

9. Who scored 60 points in his final NBA match for the LA Lakers in 2016?

10. Which leading British player retired from tennis in 2007, having failed to progress any further than the third round of a Grand Slam since 2004?

100. THE FINISHING POST – A FINAL MIXED BAG

1. Which current Premier League manager is Jurgen Klopp's landlord?

2. Which member of England's 2003 Rugby World Cup winning team had in 1985, as a 12-year-old, been one of twenty choristers who sang backing vocals on Tina Turner's song "We Don't Need Another Hero"?

3. In what sport has the fastest speed without mechanical assistance been achieved?

4. Whose motto is "Citius, Altius, Fortius", which is Latin for "faster, higher, stronger"?

5. Which former England goalkeeper, who died in April 2020, in retirement ran a guest house on the Isle of Mull and worked there as a postman?

6. In what sport would a "racing homer" be competing?

7. Who scored 153 against India at Kolkata in 1982, bowled right and left handed in the Indian innings in the same game and, on the rest day, recorded a hole in one at the local golf course?

8. What disturbance in the crowd caused a delay in the Masters Snooker final between Stuart Bingham and Ali Carter in January 2020?

9. From what sport do we get the expression "to keep tabs on"?

10. And appropriately to finish with in the context of this book, which Englishman has managed the most Premier League matches?

THE ANSWERS

1. Under starter's orders – a mixed bag
1. Shane Warne, 2. Tourist Trophy, 3. Australia, 4. Trevor Brooking (scored the winning goal in the FA Cup final), 5. Alun Wyn Jones, 6. Willie Carson, 7. Nico Hulkenberg, 8. Discus throwing, 9. Michael Chang, 10. Aston Villa.

2. Life on the ocean waves
1. Wendell Sailor, 2. Brighton and Southend, 3. The Coral Cup, 4. Beach Volleyball, 5 Dave Sands, 6. Anchor Bridge, 7. Sale Sharks, 8. Otis Ferry, 9. Craig Stadler, 10. Miami Dolphins.

3. The luck of the Irish
1.Alex Higgins, 2. Katie Taylor, 3. Brian O'Driscoll, 4. Vincent O'Brien, 5. Stephen Roche, 6. Henry Shefflin, 7. Royal Portrush, 8. Sir Anthony McCoy, 9. Conor McGregor, 10. George Best.

4. When the saints go marching in
1. Ian St John, 2. Zach Johnson, 3. Paul Grayson (he scored 2,786 points for Northampton, 131 more than Stephen Myler), 4. St Louis, Missouri, 5. St Helens Rugby League team, 6. San Jose, 7. St Leo, 8. St Paddy, 9. Recreation Ground at St Johns in Antigua, 10. Perth.

5. View from the stands
1. Polo. 2. Football (Livingston FC). 3. Boxing. 4. Bowling. 5. Horse racing (Chester). 6. Cycling (Southampton). 7. Football (Lewes FC). 8. Golf. 9. Cricket (Hampshire). 10. Rugby league (Castleford).

6. Up the garden path
1. Dickie Bird, 2. Twickenham, 3. Pool, 4. Maureen Flowers, 5. John Stones, 6. Larkspur, 7. The Shed, 8. The Robins, 9. Andy Flower, 10. David Vine.

7. Keeping up with the Joneses
1. Bobby Jones, 2. Alun Wyn Jones, 3. Dean Jones, 4. Vinnie Jones, 5. Lewis Jones, 6. Cliff Jones, 7. Jade Jones, 8. Alan Jones, 9. Geraint Jones, 10. Ann Jones.

8. Food glorious food
1. Allan Lamb, 2. John Curry, 3. Crisp, 4. Meadowlark Lemon, 5. Bread of Heaven, 6. Pat Rice, 7. Willi Heinz, 8. A Pasty, 9. Graham Onions, 10. Black Caviar.

9. The French connection
1. Georges Carpentier, 2. Snowboarding, 3. Yves Saint-Martin, 4. Eric Cantona, 5. Jacques Anquetil, 6. Jean-Claude Killy, 7. Francoise Durr, 8. Didier Deschamps, 9. Cricket, 10. Jean-Pierre Rives.

10. I was there (Paul's own reminiscences)
1. Stuart Broad, 2. Mansfield Town, 3. John Brain, 4. Hyde Park, 5. 60, 6. Tommy Hutchison, 7. The WACA at Perth, 8. Monbeg Dude, 9. Widnes and Wakefield Trinity, 10. Ted Hill.

11. Like father like son
1. Peter and Kasper Schmeichel, 2. Derek Quinnell, 3. Dan Skelton, 4. Eidur Gudjohnsen, 5. Gianfranco Dettori (his son Frankie is Lanfranco), 6. Harry Redknapp and Frank Lampard, 7. Andy and Owen Farrell, 8. Old Tom and Young Tom Morris, 9. Jack and Brian London, 10. Stanley Matthews.

12. Weights and measures
1. An ice hockey puck, 2. Sumo wrestling, 3. 22 (on the metrication of Rugby Union laws, the 25-yard line became the 22-metre line, even though the metric equivalent of 25 yards is actually closer to 23 metres), 4. Dennis Lillee, 5. Polo (the playing field is 300 x 160 yards or 270 x 150 metres), 6. Twelve feet, 7. 7ft 1in, 8. Fourteen, 9. Table tennis, 10. 9 stones.

13. First impressions
1. Eddy Merckx, 2. Ben Curtis, 3. Jonathan Woodgate, 4. Jimmy Greaves, 5. Terry Griffiths, 6. They each scored a century in their first Test match and never played in another one, 7. Jeremy Guscott, 8. Keith Deller, 9. Sport climbing and surfing, 10. Bob Massie.

14. Genuine all-rounders
1. Fred Perry, 2. Willie Davenport, 3. Christian Wade, 4. Jim Standen, 5. Jackie Stewart, 6. Lottie Dod, 7. Curtis Woodhouse, 8. JWHT Douglas, 9. Eddie Eagan, 10. Peter Cech.

15. For those watching in black and white
1. Croquet, 2. White, 3. Harlequins, 4. King of the mountains, 5. Black and white, 6. Green, 7. Red Rum, 8. Tiger Woods, 9. Green (Plymouth Argyle), 10. Squash.

16. Giant killers and underdogs
1. Belo Horizonte, 2. Paul Lawrie, 3. Kenya, 4. Goran Ivanisevic, 5. Tony Knowles, 6. Nortons Coin, 7. Greece, 8. Yorkshire, 9. James "Buster" Douglas, 10. Eddie The Eagle.

17. Aussie rules
1. Dawn Fraser, 2. Don Bradman, 3. Herb Elliott, 4. Phar Lap, 5. Jack Brabham, 6. Mal Meninga, 7. Jason Crump, 8. Margaret Court, 9. Mark Schwarzer, 10. Peter Thomson.

18. Passport control
1. Muhammad Ali, born Cassius Clay, 2. Dav Whatmore, 3. Terry Butcher, 4. Sam Underhill, 5. Bradley Wiggins, 6. Greg Rusedski, 7. Justin Rose, 8. Mo Farah, 9. Ted Dexter, 10. Matthew Le Tissier.

19. Take your partners
1. Todd Woodbridge and Mark Woodforde, 2. Irina Rodnina, 3. Fanny Sunesson, 4. Ian St John and Jimmy Greaves, 5. Tony Nash and Robin Dixon, 6. Ferenc Puskas and Alfredo Di Stefano, 7. Gordon Greenidge and Desmond Haynes, 8. Steve Redgrave and Matthew Pinsent, 9. Arkle and Pat Taaffe, 10. Jayne Torvill.

20. Holy orders
1. Nick Easter, 2. Dan Christian, 3. Thomas Lord, 4. Dixie Dean, 5. St Louis Cardinals, 6. Steve Parish, 7. Franklin's Gardens (Northampton), 8. Gabriel Jesus, 9. Ollie Pope, 10. Rob Cross.

21. Face the music
1. Muhammad Ali, 2. Snooker Loopy, 3. All I want for Christmas Is a Dukla Prague away kit, 4. Matthew Maynard, 5. Max Boyce, 6. Frank Bruno, 7. A racehorse, 8. Gerry and the Pacemakers, 9. Hulk Hogan, 10. Peter Knowles.

22. Christian names as surnames
1. Rob Andrew, 2. Ezzard Charles, 3. Bobby George, 4. Henry Paul, 5. Devon Malcolm, 6. Richard Patrick, 7. Maurice Norman, 8. Desmond Douglas, 9. Payne Stewart, 10. Josephine Gordon.

23. Surnames as Christian names
1. Stewart Cink, 2. Malcolm Marshall, 3. George Foreman, 4. Andrew Thornton, 5. Norman Whiteside, 6. Gordon D'Arcy, 7. Patrick Rafter, 8. Charles Atlas, 9. Sir Paul McCartney, 10. Douglas Scott.

24. Mamma mia
1. Sergio Parisse, 2. Alberto Ascari, 3. Fabio Capello, 4. Franceso Molinari, 5. Alberto Tomba, 6. Fiona May, 7. Gianluigi Buffon, 8. Valentino Rossi, 9. Ferrari, 10. Primo Carnera.

25. Another door opens
1. Tony O'Reilly, 2. Christine Lagarde, 3. Ray Wilson, 4. Rene Lacoste, 5. Gerald Ford, 6. Vitali Klitschko, 7. David Sheppard, 8. Phil Vickery – the Raging Bull, 9. Menzies Campbell, 10. Lee Bowyer.

26. Rogues and villains
1. Chicago White Sox, 2. Dean Richards, 3. OJ Simpson, 4. Lester Piggott, 5. Lance Armstrong, 6. Tonya Harding, 7. Peter Shilton, 8. Chris Lewis, 9. Fencing, 10. Hansie Cronje.

27. Job descriptions
1. Bill Glazier, 2. Roscoe Tanner, 3. Henry Cooper, 4. Farokh Engineer, 5. Bill Shoemaker, 6. Joe Baker, 7. Wilt Chamberlain, 8. Alastair Cook, 9. Kevin Painter, 10. George Foreman.

28. Ten to one
1. Six, 2. Ten, 3. Two, 4. Three, 5. Nine, 6. One, 7. Five, 8. Eight, 9. Four, 10. Seven.

29. Cash is king
1. Malcom MacDonald, 2. The Oval Cricket Ground, now the Kia Oval, 3. Steinlager, 4. Rod Laver, 5. Moneyball, 6. Galileo, 7. Curtis Strange, 8. Littlewoods, 9. Rowing, 10. Nike.

30. Where in the country
1. Ross County, 2. Exeter, 3. Yorkshire, 4. Ian Woosnam, 5. The Hawthorns (West Bromwich Albion), 6. The Solent, 7. Southport, 8. Junko Tabei, 9. Plymouth Hoe, 10. Cleeve Hill.

31. Lessons from history and literature
1. Anne Boleyn, 2. Arsenal, 3. Wimbledon, 4. The Pickwick Papers, 5. Billiards, 6. King Henry V, 7 Sir Arthur Conan Doyle, 8. Sebastian Coe, 9. Ten, 10. Tennis Balls.

32. The American dream
1. Dick Fosbury, 2. Michael Phelps, 3. Andre Agassi, 4. Michael Jordan, 5. Bob Beamon, 6. Megan Rapinoe, 7. Mario Andretti, 8. Brooks Koepka, 9. Pete Dawkins, 10. Brad Friedel.

33. Towns and cities in the UK
1. Allan Wells, 2. Ian Salisbury, 3. Sir Francis Chichester, 4. Justin Edinburgh, 5. Dan Biggar, 6. David Bedford, 7. Frank Chester, 8. Angelo Dundee, 9. John Buckingham, 10. Stuart Lancaster.

34. Over the hills and far away
1. Germany and Austria, 2. Jessica Ennis-Hill, 3. Nottingham Forest, 4. Box Hill, 5. Nico and Keke Rosberg, 6. Norway, 7. Richard Hill, 8. Biggin Hill, 9. A Double Gloucester Cheese, 10. Ron Hill.

35. Brotherly love
1. Manu Tuilagi, 2. Alistair and Jonny Brownlee, 3. Bob and Mike Bryan, 4. Mitchell Starc, 5. Rob, Jean-Luc and Dan Du Preez, 6. Adam and Ben Hollioake, 7. Frank and Ronald de Boer, 8. Sir Bobby and Jack Charlton, 9. Michael and Ralf Schumacher, 10. Peyton and Eli Manning.

36. The numbers board
1. One hundred and seventy, 2. Twenty-six, 3. Eighteen, 4. Nineteen, 5. Twenty-four, 6. Seventy-one (3 x 24, less Bury!), 7. Forty-seven, 8. Thirty-one, 9. Thirty, 10. 1246.

37. It's a dog's life
1 Mick the Miller, 2 Pickles, 3 Ray Pointer, 4 The Doggett's Coat and Badge, 5 The Greyhound, 6 Jack Russell, 7 Towcester, 8 The British Bulldog, 9 Collie, 10 Goodwood.

38. The Smiths
1. Harvey Smith, 2. Louis Smith, 3. Tommie Smith, 4. C Aubrey Smith, 5. Ed Smith, 6. Tommy (Crompton) Smith, 7. Callum, Liam, Paul and Stephen Smith, 8. Alan Smith, 9. David Smith, 10. His name is simply "Smith".

39. Captain Marvels
1. Richie McCaw, 2. Douglas Jardine, 3. Billy Wright and Bobby Moore, 4. Alan Prescott, 5. Eiffel Tower, 6. Willie John McBride, 7. Harry Kane, 8. Sir Henry Cooper and Cliff Morgan, 9. Emlyn Hughes, 10. Captain Christy.

40. Compass points
1. George North, 2. Orienteering, 3. West Ham United, 4. Russell Crowe, 5. Western Roll, 6. Sam Northeast, 7. George Eastham, 8. Peter West, 9. Church steeples, 10. Ray East.

41. The silver screen
1. Boxing, 2. Cool Runnings, 3. The Pie, 4. Chariots of Fire – Harold Abrahams and Eric Liddell, 5. Ipswich Town, 6. The Hustler, 7. Rugby League, 8. Octopussy, 9. The Wrestler, 10. Rollerball.

42. Hot streaks
1. Johnny Weissmuller, 2. Jahangir Khan, 3. Phil Taylor, 4. Sir Gordon Richards, 5. Australia,

6. Harlem Globetrotters, 7. Iolanda Balas, 8. Floyd Mayweather Jnr, 9. Winx, 10. Watford.

43. I can never do cryptic crosswords
1. Troy, 2. Gary Player, 3. David Coleman, 4. Chris and Stuart Broad, 5. Ivan Mauger, 6. Billy Twelvetrees, 7 Peter 'Snakebite' Wright, 8. Gary Sprake, 9. David Constant, 10. Ray Reardon.

44. Cackhanders
1. Maureen Connolly, 2. Kumar Sangakkara, 3. Hockey and polo, 4. Babe Ruth, 5. James Wade, 6. Bob Charles, 7. Tony Meo, 8. Lin Dan, 9. Rangana Herath, 10. Rafael Nadal.

45. Keep your head above water
1. Ted Heath (Sir Edward Heath), 2. Captain Matthew Webb, 3. Holme Pierrepont, Nottingham, 4. Water Polo, 5. Katharine Grainger, 6. River Tay, 7. Fulham (Craven Cottage), 8. Whitewater Slalom, 9. Coniston Water, 10. Adam Peaty.

46. Ten managers to have won Premier League
Alex Ferguson, Kenny Dalglish, Arsène Wenger, José Mourinho, Carlo Ancelotti, Roberto Mancini, Manuel Pellegrini, Claudio Ranieri, Antonio Conte, Pep Guardiola.

47. Last ten winners of the Open Golf championship
Shane Lowry, Francesco Molinari, Jordan Spieth, Henrik Stenson, Zach Johnson, Rory McIlroy, Phil Mickelson, Ernie Els, Darren Clarke, Louis Oosthuizen.

48. Ten Britons to have won F1 drivers' championship
Mike Hawthorn, Graham Hill, Jim Clark, John Surtees, Jackie Stewart, James Hunt, Nigel Mansell, Damon Hill, Lewis Hamilton, Jenson Button.

49. Last ten cities to host Summer Olympics
Rio de Janeiro, London, Beijing, Athens, Sydney, Atlanta, Barcelona, Seoul, Los Angeles, Moscow.

50. Top ten Test run scorers

Sachin Tendulkar	15,921
Ricky Ponting	13,378
Jacques Kallis	13,289
Rahul Dravid	13,288
Alistair Cook	12,472
Kumar Sangakkara	12,400
Brian Lara	11,953
Shivnarine Chanderpaul	11,867
Mahela Jayawardene	11,814
Allan Border	11,174

51. Top ten NH jockeys 19-20

	Wins
Brian Hughes	141
Richard Johnson	122
Sam Twiston-Davies	99
Harry Skelton	97
Harry Cobden	83
Aidan Coleman	82
Nico de Boinville	73
Gavin Sheehan	70
Adam Wedge	65
Jonjo O'Neill Jr	61

52. Top ten basketball scorers

Kareem Abdul-Jabbar	38,387
Karl Malone	36,928
Lebron James	34,087
Kobe Bryant	33,643
Michael Jordan	32,292
Dirk Nowitzki	31,560
Wilt Chamberlain	31,419
Shaquille O'Neal	28,596
Moses Malone	27,409
Elvin Hayes	27,313

53. Top ten Prem try scorers

Tom Varndell	92
Mark Cueto	90
Chris Ashton	86
Christian Wade	82
Steve Hanley	75
Paul Sackey	69
Matt Banahan	68
Tom Voyce	66
Jonny May	65
James Simpson-Daniel	63

54. Last ten women to win BBC Sports Personality of the Year.
Zara Phillips, Kelly Holmes, Paula Radcliffe, Liz McColgan, Fatima Whitbread, Jayne Torvill, Virginia Wade, Mary Peters, Princess Anne, Ann Jones.

55. Last ten multiple winners of Wimbledon in the Open era
Roger Federer, Pete Sampras, Novak Djokovic, Björn Borg, John McEnroe, Boris Becker, Jimmy Connors, Stefan Edberg, Rafael Nadal, Andy Murray.

56. No man is an island
1. Isle of Man, 2. Happy Valley, 3. Bermuda, 4. Faroe Islands, 5. Gibraltar, 6. Alderney, 7. Jersey, 8. Tonga, 9. Isle of Wight (at Newclose Cricket Ground), 10. Ailsa Craig.

57. Land of my fathers
1. Colin Jackson, 2. Carl Llewellyn, 3. Richard Meade, 4. Joe Calzaghe, 5. Tanni Grey-Thompson, 6. Paul Thorburn, 7. Tony Lewis, 8. Gareth Bale, 9. Ffos Las, 10. Dai Rees.

58. Where would you be?
1. The Old Course at St Andrews, 2. Kilmarnock, 3. Badminton Horse Trials, 4. Stradey Park, 5. Silverstone, 6. Ascot, 7. The Serpentine in Hyde Park, 8. Monaco, 9. Coursing, 10. Headingley.

59. More genuine all-rounders
1. Rebecca Romero, 2. Sonny Bill Williams, 3. Babe Zaharias, 4. Kevin O'Flanagan, 5. Jaroslav Drobny, 6. John Young, 7. Chris Balderstone, 8. Alex Zanardi, 9. CB Fry, 10. Geoff Capes.

60. Turn of the century
1. Cathy Freeman, 2. Kevin Phillips, 3. Marcus Trescothick, 4. Ruby Walsh, 5. Venus Williams, 6. Pebble Beach, 7. No winner is now recorded. Lance Armstrong was originally declared winner, but was stripped of this and other Tour wins in 2012, 8. Diego Dominguez, 9. Ben Ainslie, 10. Germany.

61. Initials for sporting phrases
1. 147 Maximum Break in Snooker, 2. 7 Points for a Try With Conversion, 3. 9 Dart Finish, 4. 1954 First Sub Four Minute Mile, 5. 3 Under Par is an Albatross, 6. 400 Highest Test Score, 7. 1780 First running of The Derby, 8. 5.5 Weight of Shuttlecock in Grams, 9. 1 Point for Behind in Australian Rules Football, 10. 4358 Winners Ridden by Tony McCoy.

62. The silver screen – the sequel
1. Sandra Bullock, 2. Robert Redford, 3. Rob Brydon, 4. Jake LaMotta, 5. Jonah Lomu, 6. Munich in 1972, 7. Bob Hope, 8. Aldaniti, 9. Chris Evert, 10. The Edge.

63. Injury time
1. Edgbaston, 2. Dave Beasant, 3. Metatarsal, 4. Sam Torrance, 5. Serena Williams, 6. Derek Pringle, 7. Alex Stepney, 8. He put his hand through a fence and got bitten by a lion, 9. Fred Titmus, 10. Bert Trautmann.

64. Auf wiedersehen pet
1. Roland Matthes, 2. Boris Becker, 3. Uwe Seeler, 4. Baron Gottfried von Cramm, 5. Hans Gunter Winkler, 6. Martin Kaymer, 7. Max Schmeling, 8. Heike Drechsler, 9. Jurgen Klopp, 10. Miroslav Klose.

65. Around the house
1. The Refrigerator, 2. Tony and Matt Windows, 3. James Slipper, 4. Usain Bolt, 5. The Chair, 6. Mats (Wilander), 7. Bath, 8. Mervyn Kitchen, 9. Carpet bowls, 10. Pat Cash.

66. The commentator's curse
1. Brian Johnston, 2. Sid Waddell, 3. John Dawes, 4. Dan Maskell, 5. Barry Davies, 6. Francis Lee, 7. Sid Lowe, 8. Norway, 9. Alberto Juantorena, 10. Kenneth Wolstenholme in 1966.

67. The sporting dictionary
1. Trampolining, 2. Curling, 3. Croquet, 4. Basketball and Netball, 5. Yachting, 6. Ten Pin Bowling, 7. Ice Hockey, 8. Clay Pigeon Shooting, 9. Judo, 10. Horse Racing.

68. And in the beginning
1. Hank Aaron, 2. Anthony Joshua, 3. Joe Solomon, 4. Charlie Adam, 5. Trevor Eve, 6. Wayne Daniel, 7. Jonah Burger, 8. Tammy Abraham, 9. Yannick Noah, 10. Ed Moses.

69. Ancient and modern
1. Nadia Comaneci, 2. Martina Hingis, 3. Fred Davis, 4. Seventeen, 5. Fifty-two, 6. Wilfred Benitez, 7. Shooting, 8. Sergio Garcia, 9. John Burridge, 10. Dick Saunders.

70. Scotland the brave
1. Willie Carson, 2. Mike Denness, 3. Jim Clark, 4. Curling, 5. Sandy Lyle, 6. Colin McRae, 7. Ian Black, 8. One for Arthur, 9. American football, 10. Larch.

71. Sporting disasters
1. Ayrton Senna, 2. Munich 1972, 3. Heysel, 4. Happy Valley, Hong Kong, 5. Tommy Simpson, 6. Munich, 7. Matthew Harding, 8. Le Mans, 9. Manny Mercer, 10. Phillip Hughes.
72. Keep it in the family
1. Serena and Venus Williams, 2. John and Sheila Wilcox (Waddington), 3. Becky and Ellie Downie, 4. Diane and Rosalind Rowe, 5. Gary Moore, 6. Bill McLaren, 7. Beryl and Denise Burton, 8. Nikita Parris, 9. Katie Walsh, 10. Elena Baltacha.
73. Did it really happen?
1. Jerzy Szczakiel, 2. Mark Cox and Bobby Wilson, 3. Real Tennis, 4. The Moon, 5. Derek Dooley, 6. Bertie Buse, 7. Willie John McBride, 8. Angers and Hethersett, 9. Danny O'Sullivan, 10. Jim Peters.
74. Down on the farm
1. The Milk Cup, 2. Harrow, 3. Giant Haystacks, 4. Mike Bull, 5. Wimbledon, 6. The Greyhound Derby, 7. Meadow Lane, 8. Turkey, 9. Bill Gates, 10. Cow Corner.
75. Central Europe
1 Franz Klammer, 2 Hungary, 3 Olga Korbut, 4 St Moritz, 5 Bartosz Zmarzlik, 6 Jan Zelezny, 7 Martina Navratilova, 8 Victor Barna, 9 Gil Merrick, 10 Emil Zatopek.
76. Can't see the wood for the trees
1. The Oaks, 2. Trevor Cherry, 3. Holly, 4. Pinetree, 5. Mike Hawthorn, 6. Fir Park, 7. Newlands, Cape Town, 8. Toronto Maple Leafs, 9. Tiger Woods, 10. John Sherwood.
77. Pipped at the post
1. India, 2. Teddy Sheringham and Ole Gunnar Solskjaer, 3. Rory McIlroy, 4. Felipe Massa, 5. Al Boum Photo, 6. Mike Catt, 7. Alan Wells and Mike McFarlane, 8. Atlanta Falcons, 9. Don Fox, 10. Jason Roy.
78. The wheel of fortune
1. Sir Chris Hoy, 2. Le Mans, 3. Champs Elysees, 4. Aintree, 5. Stock Car Racing, 6. Tai Woffinden, 7. David Weir, 8. Michael Schumacher, 9. Indianapolis 500, 10. John Surtees.
79. Top of the class
1. Charterhouse, 2. Cheltenham College, 3. Eton Fives, 4. Rugby, 5. Millfield, 6. Clifton College, 7. Owen Farrell and George Ford, 8. Hogwarts, 9. Harrow, 10. Whitgift – Dominic Sibley, Rory Burns and Jason Roy.
80. The Spanish inquisition
1. Marc Marquez, 2. Miguel Indurain, 3. Arantxa Sanchez Vicario, 4. Seve Ballesteros, 5. Pep Guardiola, 6. Carlos Sainz, 7. El Cordobes, 8. Fernando Alonso, 9. Kane, 10. Andres Iniesta.
81. Way back in time
1. 1,000 Guineas, 2. Athens (in 1896), 3. Rugby League, 4. Wimbledon Tennis, 5. WL 'Billy' Murdoch 6. Henley on Thames, 7. Blackheath, 8. Notts County, 9. Marquess of Queensbury Rules, 10. Prestwick.
82. Gone fishin'
1. Charlton Athletic, 2. Kemar Roach, 3. David Sole, 4. Greg Norman, 5. Pike, 6. Mike Trout, 7. Jack Dempsey, 8. Rob Herring, 9. David Bass, 10. Eric the Eel.
83. Film/TV – the name's the same
1. Richard / Mark Todd, 2. Ronnie / James J Corbett, 3. Emma / Bubba Watson, 4. Richard / Mike Burton, 5. Anthony / Eamonn Andrews, 6. Arthur / John Lowe, 7. Albert / Tom Finney, 8. Daniel / Paula Radcliffe, 9. Peter / Tony Kay, 10. Fiona / Simon Shaw.
84. Marital bliss
1. Robbie Brightwell, 2. Ellyse Perry, 3. Hockey, 4. Terry Biddlecombe, 5. Mike and Zara Tindall, 6. Greg Norman, 7. Simon Easterby, 8. Ten (Jason 6, Laura 4), 9. Mitchell Starc, 10. Hugh Porter.
85. "And I quote"
1. George Best, 2. Douglas Jardine, 3. Mick Fitzgerald, 4. Gary Player, 5. Keith Miller, 6. Bill Shankly, 7. Nigel Owens, 8. Phil Tufnell, 9. Lee Trevino, 10. Brian Clough.

86. The drinks cabinet
1. Charlotte Brew, 2. Frank and Percy Stout, 3. Vladimir Smirnov, 4. Sherry's Prince, 5. Squash, 6. Dick Advocaat, 7. Jannie de Beer, 8. Pierluigi Martini, 9. Phil Mead, 10. The Claret Jug.

87. Strange but true
1. Geoff Griffin, 2. Ronnie Simpson, 3. Lorenzo Bandini, 4. Jack Johnson, 5. JPR Williams, 6. Billy Griffiths, 7. Ian Hall, 8. Fencing, 9. Martin Molony, 10. Ben Hogan.

88. Your satnav may help
1. f. CT13 9PB Royal St George's, Sandwich, 2. g. BD6 1BS Odsal Stadium, Bradford, 3. j. SA2 0AR St Helen's, Swansea, 4. c. S1 1DA The Crucible, Sheffield, 5. k. CB8 8EP Newmarket, 6. h. YO23 1EX York, 7. e. LE2 7TR Welford Road, Leicester, 8. a. G40 3HG Glasgow, 9. d. NE1 4ST Newcastle upon Tyne, 10. b. EX4 6PX Exeter.

89. The nobility
1. Emily Davison, 2. Rajasthan Royals, 3. Mary King, 4. Anthony Armstrong-Jones, 5. Queen of the South, 6. Badminton, 7. Dick Francis, 8. Crown Green Bowls, 9. Princess Anne and Zara Tindall, 10. Prince Alexander Obolensky.

90. I was there (Chris's own reminiscences)
1. Liverpool, 2. Ray Wood, 3. Richard Sharp, 4. Linford Christie, 5. Kauto Star, 6. A bowler of high-flighted non spinning leg breaks with the initials CC, 7. Oliver McCall, 8. The Tavern, 9. Stephen Fry, 10. Peter Wilson.

91. The Met office
1. Toby Flood, 2. Western Storm, 3. Rubin "Hurricane" Carter, 4. Many Clouds, 5. Bryony Frost, 6. John Snow, 7. Tony Gale, 8. Buxton, 9. Early Mist, 10. The Iceman (Kimi Raikkonen).

92. Mrs Brown's boys
1. Ken Brown, 2. Veronica Campbell-Brown, 3. Bill Brown, 4. Sky Brown, 5. Dougie Brown, 6. Antonio Brown, 7. Inge De Bruijn, 8. Mike Brown, 9. Danielle Brown, 10. Joe Brown.

93. London calling
1. Brentford, 2. Romford and Crayford, 3. Removing the bails from the wicket, 4. Ball and mallet (a possible forerunner of croquet), 5. Hampton Court, 6. White City, 7. Boston Red Sox v New York Yankees, 8. Trailfinders Sports Ground in Ealing, 9. The Oval, 10. Wasps.

94. Out of Africa
1. Kip Keino, 2. Siya Kolisi, 3. Jody Scheckter, 4. Kirsty Coventry, 5. Basel, 6. Haile Gebrselassie, 7. Gary Player, 8. John Isner, 9. Clive Van Ryneveld, 10. Kinshasa.

95. I can see clearly now
1. David Steele, 2. Dennis Taylor, 3. Edgar Davids, 4. Hale Irwin, 5. Shane Warne, 6. Billie Jean King, 7. David Bryant, 8. Ian McKinley, 9. Jack Leach, 10. Sydney Wooderson.

96. The Queen's coronation year
1. Stanley Mortenson, 2. Carl 'Bobo' Olsen, 3. Ben Hogan, 4. Ice dancing, 5. Sir John Hunt, 6. Geoff Duke, 7. Sir Gordon Richards, 8. The Queen, 9. Len Hutton, 10. Ken Rosewall.

97. When there was still sport in 2020
1. Jill Scott, 2. Rafael Nadal, 3. Jonjo O'Neill junior, 4. Dominic Sibley, 5. Charles Ollivon with four, 6. Australia, 7. Stevenage, 8. Simon Harmer, 9. Elinor Barker, 10. Jonathan Davies.

98. The NHS
1. Rugby union, 2. The Fremantle Doctor, 3. Dr Renee Richards, 4. Dr Benjamin Spock, 5. Seymour Nurse, 6. Brian Lima, 7. Dr Devious, 8. Danny Nightingale, 9. John Landy, 10. Greg Hancock.

99. The last goodbyes
1. Jack Nicklaus, 2. Ayr, 3. Mike Tindall, 4. John Arlott, 5. Rocky Marciano (Marchegiano), 6. Exeter, 7. Alastair Cook, 8. Sergio Parisse, 9. Kobe Bryant, 10. Tim Henman.

100. The finishing post – a mixed bag
1. Brendan Rogers, 2. Lawrence Dallaglio, 3. Downhill skiing, 4. Olympic Games, 5. Peter Bonetti, 6. Pigeon racing, 7. Graham Gooch, 8. Someone using a "whoopee cushion", 9. Archery, 10. He wrote the foreword, so we'll give him the last word: Harry Redknapp!